# Spiritual Breakthroughs:

## A Bible-Based Approach to Making and Sustaining Difficult Changes

by Monte Drenner

PRESS

*Spiritual Breakthroughs*
*A Bible-Based Approach to Making and Sustaining*
*Difficult Life Changes*
by Monte Drenner

Printed in the United States of America

ISBN 9781619044524

The New International Version (NIV) 1984 version of the Bible. Scripture quotations marked (NIV) are taken from the 2011 edition.

Visit www.mtccounseling.com for additional resources and more information on Spiritual Breakthroughs.

www.xulonpress.com

# Dedication

To Sandy, my awesome wife and best friend
of 30 years, your breakthroughs have helped hundreds of
others, and my own would not have been possible without
you. To my incredible daughters, Christina and Kelsey,
your breakthroughs call me higher and inspire me to be a
more spiritual man. I could not be more blessed to have
the three of you in my life. Your unconditional love and
undying support mean more to me than
words can express.

# Acknowledgements

ॐ

I want to thank my amazing editor Laura Rabell.
Your spiritual approach, insights, and incredible way with
words made this God project possible. I could not have
done this without you.

To all the men in my life throughout the years
who have helped me make the spiritual breakthroughs
I desperately wanted and needed to make, your love for
God, His word, and His Kingdom have inspired and
guided me to become more like Jesus. You all
have my undying gratitude.

# About the Author
## Monte Drenner

Upon graduation from the University of Florida
in 1980, Monte served for seven years as a U.S. Army
Intelligence Officer. He and his wife, Sandy, served in the
ministry for 16 years in non-denominational churches
in the Southeast. In 2003 they moved to the Orlando,
Florida, area and established More Than Conquerors
(MTC) Counseling. In addition to a spiritual background
in counseling, Monte holds a Master's degree in Mental
Health Counseling and is also a Certified Addictions
Professional. Monte has vast experience counseling
individuals, couples, and families with complex mental
health and substance abuse issues. He also provides
spiritual life coaching, offers staff training, and conducts
church workshops on spiritual growth and other topics.
Monte and Sandy recently celebrated their 30th wedding
anniversary and have two adult daughters who
reside in Charlotte, NC.

# Table of Contents

❦

**INTRODUCTION – SPIRITUAL
BREAKTHROUGH DEFINED** ........................... xiii

**PART I – SPIRITUAL BREAKTHROUGH** ........... 19

Chapter 1: Going Through the Motions ............................ 21
Chapter 2: Religious vs. Spiritual ............................ 28
Chapter 3: Becoming More Spiritual ........................ 37
Chapter 4: The Spirit ............................ 49
Chapter 5: The Foundation for Breakthroughs ................ 59
Chapter 6: The Approach ............................ 73
Chapter 7: Interventions ............................ 79

**PART II – CORE BELIEFS** ...................................... 87

Chapter 8: Change Your View of Change ........................ 89
Chapter 9: Change Your Expectations ........................ 95
Chapter 10: Let Go of the Status Quo ........................ 99
Chapter 11: Change Your View of Impossible .............. 107
Chapter 12: Change Your Worldview .............................. 112
Chapter 13: Obstacle or Opportunity? ........................ 122
Chapter 14: Change Your Attitude about Comfort
                and Suffering ...................................... 126

Chapter 15: Change Your Attitude about Weaknesses....135
Chapter 16: Failure Is Not Fatal ..........................................140
Chapter 17: Playing the Victim and Other Roles.............145
Chapter 18: Change Your View of You .............................156

**PART III – HOPE** ..................................................... **163**

Chapter 19: Choose Hope ....................................................165
Chapter 20: The God of Hope.............................................171
Chapter 21: Fear ....................................................................177
Chapter 22: Discouragement ..............................................184
Chapter 23: Getting Past Your Past ...................................198
Chapter 24: Guilt and Shame..............................................205
Chapter 25: Hope Deferred .................................................216

**PART IV – MOTIVATION FOR CHANGE**.......... **223**

Chapter 26: Marginal Motivators........................................225
Chapter 27: Paul's Motivation ............................................232
Chapter 28: Knowing Jesus .................................................235
Chapter 29: Understanding Reconciliation .......................245
Chapter 30: The Spiritual Lottery.......................................250
Chapter 31: The Cross .........................................................262
Chapter 32: Attitude of Gratitude .....................................269

**CONCLUSION** ..................................................... **275**

Additional Resources............................................................283

# INTRODUCTION

# Introduction

# Spiritual Breakthrough Defined

❧

"Spiritual breakthrough" and "dramatic spiritual growth" may be new terms to you. Perhaps you've never heard these phrases before, but you probably know you need to make some difficult changes, perhaps many of them. If this describes your situation, you are not alone. I find this to be true for many believers who are seeking spiritual growth. Think about the last time you made a spiritual breakthrough or experienced a significant change. For many Christians, it has been far too long. These phrases are rarely used, probably because they so rarely occur. But that's not how it has always been. The heroes of faith in the Old Testament and the apostles in the New Testament made lots of breakthroughs and experienced dramatic spiritual growth. Why, you may ask? Were they more gifted than we are? Did they have some spiritual resource not available to us today? Was it because they lived in more simple times? I don't think any of these possible explanations are true. No, I believe it was because they had different expectations for their lives. All of the Biblical characters mentioned throughout this book achieve radical transformations, but none started out as heroes or apostles. Like us, they also had to learn to banish negative thoughts, control their emotions, and break free from enslavement to certain behaviors. This scenario describes what my life was like for several years and describes the lives of millions of Christians today. These believers, like my former self, have yet to embrace the reality that they, too, can make radical changes in *any* area of their life. You may attend church with one of these believers, or perhaps you live with one. Maybe you are one, yourself. I was certainly one of them. Working with believers from all walks of life has convinced me there are far too many Christians having breakdowns and too few experiencing breakthroughs.

But what exactly is a spiritual breakthrough? For the purposes of this book, a spiritual breakthrough is *"an obvious and observable change in controlling thoughts, feelings, or behaviors, resulting in dramatic spiritual growth."* The bottom line is, when you make a spiritual breakthrough, it will be obvious. You will know it, and others will see it, too. Making *and* sustaining spiritual breakthroughs will transform you into a drastically different person. That is what the power of God can do if we *allow* it. Yes, you read that correctly; we must *allow* the most powerful force in the universe to work in our lives. We can stop the power of God simply by deciding not to change. I made the decision to hinder His power many times in the past, and perhaps you are making it right now. My prayer is that by picking up this book, you made the first step towards opening your heart and mind to the power of God and are ready to delve into His Scriptures.

The Apostle Paul was radically transformed and offers this commentary on his life prior to becoming a Christian:

*It is for freedom that Christ has set us free. Stand firm, then, and do not let yourselves be burdened again by a yoke of slavery.*
Galatians 5:1

Before becoming a Christian, Paul *was* a slave to sin. This statement is true for all believers. Before becoming a Christian, there is no question that I was powerless over worldly thoughts, had difficultly controlling certain emotions, and was enslaved to sinful behaviors. Unfortunately, there were also times I lived an anemic Christian life. You, too, may be living one right now. How does this impotent life occur? Like the Hebrew slaves who were freed during the exodus, I brought the mind of a slave into a new and free life. My failures at living a victorious Christian life in the past occurred because the mind of a slave also accompanies a heart of fear. God wants those He frees today to be empowered to change in *every* area of our lives. God wants His children to understand that we no longer need to be enslaved to the things that held us captive before becoming Christians. As His children, God wants us to embrace the idea that Jesus did not come just to free us from the consequences of sin but to make us more than conquerors over sin.

Thriving spiritually is now my goal rather than just surviving. I am at the stage in my life where I *really* want to grow spiritually. As I matured as a Christian, I became tired of giving into fear, settling for mediocrity, going through the motions, and being powerless over certain things in my life. Perhaps you are, too. I now understand that being transformed more into the likeness of Christ is *always* God's plan for us and comes as a result of making *and* sustaining multiple spiritual breakthroughs. In the past, I failed to make spiritual breakthroughs and experience dramatic spiritual growth because I lacked an understanding of God's vision for me and hope that I could change. Many believers today are in this same situation. Throughout this book, I will explain Biblical concepts in a simple manner and help you apply them to your life. Whatever your current spiritual condition, I can relate, and this book will help you achieve the spiritual growth you seek. This book was inspired by the men and women of the Bible who were radically transformed, my own spiritual breakthroughs, and hundreds of believers who have implemented these godly principles presented in God's instruction manual for His people. My prayer for you now is that you will open your heart to God's word, His vision for your life, and His power as you move forward on your journey of continual transformation into the likeness of Christ.

# PART I

# SPIRITUAL
# BREAKTHROUGH

## Chapter 1

# Going Through the Motions

*And you, my son Solomon, acknowledge the God of your father, and serve him with wholehearted devotion and with a willing mind, for the LORD searches every heart and understands every motive behind the thoughts.*
I Chronicles 28:9a

A sad but true reality is that far too many believers in Jesus are not living the abundant life He promised. Many believers *endure* their Christian life rather than *enjoy* it, a spiritual existence, but not spiritual excellence. If this describes you, I feel your pain. For many years, I lived in a spiritual no man's land. I was living neither a satisfactory Christian life nor a fulfilled worldly life. I had a pulse but not much passion. In many ways, I was simply going through the motions. Like Matthew West sings in his popular song, "The Motions," I needed help to fight through the nothingness of this life. I decided that just doing OK spiritually was not going to be enough.

Many believers are confronted with this same scenario, merely existing or simply going through their days as a victim of their circumstances or emotions. Enslaved to various sins, poor attitudes, pessimism, faithlessness, or negative emotions and behaviors, others are merely surviving life day to day. These believers often have the career or family they want but not a truly fulfilling spiritual life. Due to fear and discouragement, they resemble the Israelite nation wandering aimlessly in a desert wasteland. God met the Israelite's physical needs daily with manna, but they lacked a spiritual connection with their Creator. These slaves were focused on physical survival and not spiritual revival. Many believers today also find themselves in a similar predicament. As in Solomon's day, God is searching their hearts and minds. God is finding many of these believers to be intelligent, insightful and industrious, as He created them to be. But He also finds many of them void of spiritual wellness and full of emptiness.

Many of these believers desire to serve God wholeheartedly, but something they may not even be aware of is holding them back. Some Christians believe they don't know how to develop a closer spiritual connection with God. They often feel stuck spiritually but do not know why, attempting and failing to make difficult life changes, not just once but many times. The spiritual breakthroughs they long for are elusive, and they cannot seem to figure out how to "get it all together" spiritually. For many Christians, these failures bring them great shame and disgust because they are not accustomed to failure. Now they have compounded their problem. They do not know how to deal with failure, and they are not getting the help they need to change. The world becomes more enticing, and putting up the spiritual front is increasingly difficult. These believers, over time, can become hopeless for change and hollow, as a shell, spiritually.

You may be one of these believers who is tired of spiritual mediocrity and regrets a lack of wholehearted devotion to God. But it's unlike you to be half-hearted. So, your lack of devotion to God may be due to a lack of understanding about how to make and sustain the spiritual breakthroughs necessary to live the life you want to live. You may not even be aware there is a way out of your spiritual wasteland. You feel called out of this second-rate spirituality but cannot break from its clutches. Surprisingly, many believers who are going through the motions don't feel they are missing out on anything at all. They believe this is the way life is. They believe a phrase coined by King Solomon more than 3,000 years ago: "everything is meaningless and chasing after the wind" (Ecclesiastes 1:14). But most have yet to persevere and arrive at the wise king's conclusion:

*Now all has been heard;*
 *here is the conclusion of the matter:*
*Fear God and keep his commandments,*
 *for this is the whole duty of man.*
Ecclesiastes 12:13

As an incredible number of believers go through the motions of school, work, marriage, church, raising children and more, they find ways — often sinful, destructive and unhealthy ways — to manage the meaninglessness of life. They suppose that a certain degree, job, relationship, position in church, or something else will give them more zeal for life. Often the things they try are secret, shameful behaviors that eventually become addictive. Over time, they try many things to fill the spiritual void. These events and activities may bring temporary joy and meaning but lead to the same empty place spiritually.

Lukewarm believers lack the purpose, passion and power to live the life they want, eventually accepting the meaninglessness of life as a lifestyle. This scenario describes my life years ago. If it also describes your life, this book is for you. Keep reading to discover that there is far more to the Christian life than just going through the motions. With God, you can break out of this situation and make a spiritual breakthrough.

## Spiritually Stuck

Other believers know by experience, instinct or observation that there is a full life in Christ. However, they are often unaware of how to make or sustain the spiritual breakthroughs necessary to maintain this full life. They may attend a seminar or retreat and have a brief, reviving mountaintop emotional and spiritual experience. However, the euphoria is short-lived and soon lost when they return to the valleys of life. These believers often live their spiritual lives in pursuit of the next high they will experience on the next mountaintop.

Many Christians who make a significant change in some area of their life eventually backslide into old ways of thinking, feeling and behaving. The full life is not real for them on a continuous basis, so they accept spiritual defeat in some area of their life, having tried to change and failed too many times. They attempted to make spiritual breakthroughs in the past but, time after time, were unsuccessful to either make or sustain the breakthroughs they desperately desired. Increasingly frustrated, discouraged and even hopeless, they stop believing in the possibility of a full life in Christ. Eventually, some even become cynical and purport that this "full life" business is a myth. They may further conclude that that the Bible is full of tales and not truths. If this describes your situation, this book is also for you. This book can give you the hope, inspiration, and practical tools to equip you for the life you really want.

## New Wine in Old Skins

Many Christians are frustrated and discouraged about their lack of spiritual progress because they try to put new wine into old wineskins. This parable is recorded in Matthew 9, Mark 2, and Luke 5. The people Jesus referred to in the parable attempted to bring old ways of thinking, dealing with emotions, and behaving into a new life. My personal attempts at this approach did not work. My experience is that many Christians today have a similar approach to life. They inadvertently bring old ways of coping with an empty life into their new life in Christ. Often these believers continue to view and cope with life's stressors in the same unspiritual manner they used before becoming a Christian. This practice, too, is vanity and chasing after the wind. These Christians are in a free land but continue to think like slaves. This approach did not work for the Hebrew slaves who left Egypt and will not work for us either.

The end result compares to the fate of the mismanaged wine in the wineskins parable; the skins burst and the wine is lost. The full life that Jesus promised must be built on a different way of thinking than you had prior to becoming a Christian. This new way of thinking will lead to more positive emotions and translate into more healthy behaviors. This "new wine in old wineskins" approach is just as disastrous now as it was then; the heart and spirit break, but there are no breakthroughs.

## Follow Me

In order to enjoy the abundant life Jesus promised, we must change our approach. We must take a deeper look at what Jesus meant when He gave His disciples the command to "follow me." Following Jesus is not just a command to obey; it is a calling to embrace. This higher calling leads to transformation. Simply stated, Jesus wants to take us to spiritual heights we have never obtained. Following Jesus to these mountaintops will produce many spiritual breakthroughs. The ultimate outcome of following Jesus is becoming a more spiritual person. How do these "never been there before spiritually" events happen? As a result of following Jesus, our thinking will change. Following Jesus led Peter to believe he could walk on water. Following Jesus led Peter, James and John to a place where Jesus was transformed, and they heard the voice of God. Who wouldn't want these types of experiences? There have been times in my Christian life when I wasn't ready for the unbelievable, similar to the people Jesus called in Luke 9 who made excuses. One did not want to be bothered, another was afraid, and the last one procrastinated. All of these reasons also explain why many believers do not make spiritual breakthroughs.

Through this book, Jesus may call you to follow Him somewhere you don't want to go. He may call you to trust Him to lead you to the breakthroughs you want to make. He may be asking you, "how long will you settle for spiritual mediocrity? How long will you regret not taking advantage of yet another opportunity for change?" What will your answer be? When we truly follow Jesus, we will learn to think and perceive the world like Jesus did. This different mindset will lead us to feel differently about the things in our life causing us distress or enslaving us. We will conceive of "the impossible" in a different way. When we consider changing an addictive behavior, personality trait, deep-seated resentment, anger, way of thinking, or sin as impossible, we are not thinking like Jesus. Our way of thinking can lead to hopelessness and being spiritually stuck. His way leads to transformation.

As we follow Jesus, He will teach us the greatest command. Jesus told His followers to "Love the Lord your God with all your heart and with all your soul and with all your mind and with all your strength" (Mark 12:30). As we learn to obey this command, we will realize the condition of these aspects of ourselves. We may realize that our heart, mind and soul are damaged and need to be healed. As you read on, you will see many examples of individuals who were healed in one or more of these areas. The Apostle Paul's soul was so corrupt he could kill Christians. The Apostle John's heart was so hardened that he wanted to call down fire from heaven on people of another race. A man named Legion literally lost his mind and lived in the tombs. All of these and more are examples of the healing power of God. The help we all need is spiritual, and each of these components of our life may require breakthroughs. This book is about how to make and sustain these breakthroughs, so we can live the spiritual life we long to live.

# Chapter 2

# Religious vs. Spiritual

I am notorious for skipping over the introduction to books. If you are like me, you missed some very valuable information already. In the introduction, I defined the term "spiritual breakthrough," but I want to take some time here to elaborate more on this phrase.

First, let's explore the word "spiritual." It may surprise you to learn that the most spiritual man who ever lived never used the word. Jesus was conceived by the Spirit (Matthew 1:18), baptized with the Spirit (Matthew 3:11), descended upon by the Spirit in the form of a dove at His baptism (Matthew 3:16), and was led by the Spirit into the desert to be tempted by Satan (Matthew 4:1). Because of His relationship with the Spirit, Jesus had a great deal to say about spirituality. Millions of His followers have imitated His spiritual qualities for the past two millennia. When Jesus commands us to follow Him, He does not mean just his actions. He also means to follow His concept of spirituality. People often wonder, "What's the difference between spiritual and religious?" One of Jesus' biggest challenges was to get the people of His time to see the difference between these two concepts. Most often, His listeners did not get it;

many Christians today do not grasp the difference either. In order to be transformed into the likeness of Christ, we *must* understand the difference.

Jesus had many discussions with the religious leaders of His time about the topic of spirituality. Mark 7 provides an example of such a discussion:

*So the Pharisees and teachers of the law asked Jesus, "Why don't your disciples live according to the tradition of the elders instead of eating their food with 'unclean' hands?"*

*He replied, "Isaiah was right when he prophesied about you hypocrites; as it is written:*

*'These people honor me with their lips,*
*    but their hearts are far from me.*
*They worship me in vain;*
*    their teachings are but rules taught by men.'*

*You have let go of the commands of God and are holding on to the traditions of men."*
Mark 7:5-8

The religious leaders confronted Jesus about neglecting a particular religious tradition of the time. In response, Jesus quoted the prophet Isaiah who preceded Him by 700 years. Jesus made the point that holding on to manmade doctrines and traditions does not make one more spiritual. Jesus emphasized that true spirituality is a matter of the heart. The conversion of God's people from religious to spiritual has been a struggle for centuries. Getting people to understand the head to heart connection was a challenge for the Old Testament prophets and for Jesus as well. The same struggle exists for us today. Jesus is making the point that spirituality is about who we *are*, not just what we *do*. Keeping traditions may provide us with comfort and structure but will not necessarily make us more spiritual. Spirituality is a condition of heart and is much more about "being" than "doing." When we become a Christian, we begin a spiritual pilgrimage to imitate the heart and mind of Jesus, not just His deeds.

The bottom line is that spiritual people don't just "talk the talk;" they also "walk the walk." They know the Bible and live it out on a continuous basis. Their relationship with God is not based upon rules to keep but a desire to maintain a bond of trust and intimacy with God. In other words, their lives and their message match. Religion lacks power to change lives; whereas the Spirit empowers believers to change anything. When I started my spiritual pilgrimage, Christianity was much more about doing what Jesus did than becoming more like Him. I am a "doer" by nature, constantly in motion and almost always doing something. I feel better about myself and more productive when I am doing something. I realized, however, that becoming more spiritual requires things that I do not naturally participate in, like introspection, evaluation, meditation, and reflection. None of these are strengths of mine, but they are necessary in order to become more like Jesus. It is difficult to participate in these activities while constantly in motion. Like the Pharisees, I practiced keeping rules without changing my heart, which led to a great deal of emotional pain and spiritual decay.

### Spirituality is a Process

A process means that there is ongoing motion to an outcome. For example, pregnancy is a closed process from conception to birth. A closed process has a definitive beginning and end. Creation, on the other hand, is an open-ended process; astronomers believe that the universe is still expanding. Creation is an open-ended process because there is no real "end." Spirituality, like creation, is an open-ended process. You may just be starting your spiritual journey, or you may be well on your way in the process. Either way, you must understand that we never really "arrive" spiritually until we get to heaven.

A crucial part of this spiritual journey is learning to take control of our thoughts, emotions and behaviors. Changing each of these aspects of our lives is a process. It is important to understand the relevance of being in a process that is open-ended. In this spiritual process, you must be patient with and encourage yourself for the progress you make. If you are like me, your impatience during times of slow progress will lead to frustration and discouragement. The process sometimes moves slowly, sometimes quickly. Generally, a great deal of momentum builds before the breakthrough happens. Every step you take towards a breakthrough is important because each step leads towards that momentum. We must also understand that there are no shortcuts to spirituality. Sometimes you will make many "baby steps" before the breakthrough occurs. The important thing to acknowledge is that you are going in the right direction.

The distance and speed you travel in this spiritual process will depend upon several factors. Some of these factors you can control, and others you cannot. Years ago, I backpacked through the Appalachian Mountains and the Alps. The distance we hiked each day was a result of our physical condition, the terrain, the weather, the speed we walked, but most importantly, how much weight we carried. The lighter our pack, the farther we could travel. Presently, you may be traveling light. You may be a veteran of many spiritual journeys and may not be carrying a lot of weight from the past. If you are a spiritually healthy person, you can change a pervasive behavior or thought pattern that has mildly impaired your life in a relatively short period of time.

All breakthroughs, however, are challenging and take effort, energy, and perseverance to accomplish.

Conversely, you may be carrying very heavy packs full of negative emotions and may not be very spiritually healthy. You may have pervasive thought patterns that are causing you great distress. The speed of your breakthrough will be determined by how much baggage you are carrying and your current spiritual condition. Regardless of your current spiritual condition and your issues, God is big enough to help you change. Regardless of the "degree of difficulty" of the breakthrough you want to make, it is possible. It is not relevant or healthy to compare your breakthrough to others. We must run the race God has marked out for us. Each person's unique race has the same finish line but a different course.

## Jesus and the Process

Many Christians are surprised to learn that Jesus had to grow spirituality just as we do. The following passage iterates this truth. This passage comes from the time when Jesus' parents found Him in the temple after they accidently left Him in Jerusalem when He was twelve.

*So he went back to Nazareth with them, and lived obediently with them. His mother held these things dearly, deep within herself. And Jesus matured, growing up in both body and spirit, blessed by both God and people.*
Luke 2:51-52, MSG

Jesus grew in "body and spirit." The Son of God had to invest time, effort and energy in becoming more spiritual. The rest of us sons and daughters of God need to do the same in order grow in our relationship with the Father.

*While he lived on earth, anticipating death, Jesus cried out in pain and wept in sorrow as he offered up priestly prayers to God. Because he honored God, God answered him. Though he was God's Son, he learned trusting-obedience by what he suffered, just as we do.*
Hebrews 5:7-8a, MSG

Part of Jesus' spiritual growth was *learning* obedience. You may be surprised to learn that Jesus was not just instantly spiritual. We must understand that spirituality was a process, not an event, even for the Son of God. Most of the poor and, therefore, unspiritual decisions I have made in my life are a direct result of me not trusting God's ways and promises. Many times, I took matters into my own hands. I pursued worldly solutions to problems and suffered the consequences, yet I learned obedience from suffering these consequences. Can you relate? If so, you are in good company, and there is hope for you, too.

A crucial part of becoming more spiritual is defeating temptation. Many believers are surprised to learn that Jesus was tempted in every way we are. Thankfully, He was able to overcome each temptation and remain sinless.

*Because he himself suffered when he was tempted, he is able to help those who are being tempted.*
Hebrews 2:18

*For we do not have a high priest who is unable to sympathize with our weaknesses, but we have one who has been tempted in every way, just as we are—yet was without sin. Let us then approach the throne of grace with confidence, so that we may receive mercy and find grace to help us in our time of need.*
Hebrews 4:15-16

Spiritual people will continually learn to trust God to guide them through temptations. Right now, you may be tempted to put this book down and rationalize, yet again, why you cannot change. If these are your thoughts, this is an excellent opportunity to trust God that He will lead you to a better spiritual place. You may be tempted now to remain religious and try to become more spiritual another time. It takes little trust in God to be religious. Religious people generally trust their ability to keep the rules and not God's ability to change their life.

We also have many other Biblical examples to imitate on our journey to becoming more spiritual. Pick any hero of faith from Hebrews 11. All of these spiritual giants initially chose the same path of trusting their own ways over God's, but God used them mightily as each, in turn, learned a more spiritual approach. All of them had character flaws and sins that dominated their life, yet they are held up as heroes. Faith led them to change. Faith can lead you to change as well, so you can become a hero for someone else.

The process for growing spiritually typically follows a simple pattern. A difficult situation causes distress; the Bible refers to this situation as a trial. We ask God for deliverance from this distress. God hears us but has a purpose for the trail. That purpose, to our dismay, is to help us grow and mature spiritually. The trial is an opportunity for a breakthrough or a breakdown. We get to make the choice. Our attitude towards this process will determine the outcome. During the trial, we have the choice to trust God to deliver us His way or to take matters into our own hands. If we navigate the trial God's way, we emerge more spiritual. If we handle the trial our way, we may feel beaten down and perhaps even broken down and bitter. Most of us have multiple trials going on simultaneously. The impact of dealing with each of them in a worldly way can be devastating spiritually, emotionally, physically and psychologically. The process for spiritual growth requires experiencing trials in a manner that results in becoming more like Jesus. Whatever you are going through now can help transform you into the likeness of Christ if you trust the process.

Jesus trusted God, and therefore, He trusted the process. As Jesus grew spiritually from His trials, He developed a deeper and more intimate relationship with the Father. The foundation for any relationship is trust, so a fundamental aspect of Jesus' relationship with God was trust. A crucial component of becoming more spiritual is developing a more trusting relationship with God. It may come as a surprise to you, but Jesus had to learn this spiritual quality as well. We cannot become more like Jesus if we do not trust God. We cannot make spiritual breakthroughs if we do not grow in our trust with God. I had to make many breakthroughs in the area of trust, and you may need to as well. Jesus had such a trusting relationship with God that even His enemies acknowledged it. Those who hurled insults at Jesus on the cross said, "He trusts in God. Let God rescue him now if he wants him" (Matthew 27:43a). Jesus trusted God to the cross and beyond. As His followers, we must learn to do the same.

As we follow Jesus, we will have many opportunities to learn to trust God more. The acid test of trust is whether or not we will take over a situation from God's control. Jesus had to face this same test of trust. Jesus was rescued from the cross when He died. Jesus even trusted God in the way that He would be rescued from a difficult situation. My sinful and untrusting nature wants to take over when I cannot see how things are going to work out according to *my* plan. Yet Jesus even trusted God when he felt abandoned. Just before Jesus died, he asked, "My God, my God, why have you forsaken me?" (Matthew 27:46b). In spite of intense suffering physically, emotionally and spiritually, Jesus trusted God. How would your life be different if Jesus had stopped trusting God on the cross? How would your life be different now if you trusted God more as you go through your trials? How would the lives of those around you be different if they imitated your trust in God through trials?

As you go through the spiritual breakthrough process, you may feel physical, emotional and spiritual pain. When we feel pain of any type, we can be tempted to stop, but if we give up, we miss out on the growth that can occur. If you trust God and His promises, like Jesus, you will be delivered from trials in God's way. If you intervene and take control when things get difficult, you will not see breakthroughs. Trusting in God leads to spiritual transformation. Trusting in ourselves leads spiritual termination.

## Chapter 3

# Becoming More Spiritual

So how do we become more spiritual? One way, as we already discussed, is to imitate Jesus' approach to trials, but there are other ways, too. For the first several years of my Christian life, I was very focused on activities like going to church, reading my Bible, serving others and evangelism. Many of my spiritual activities were positive, but for me, they gradually became negative as my motive turned to gaining spiritual knowledge. Paul addressed this approach when he said, "knowledge puffs up, but love builds up" (I Corinthians 8:1). Knowledge is good, but the spiritual quality of love is the path to changing our hearts and becoming more spiritual.

At this stage of your life, you may be discouraged by your current spiritual condition. Do not be discouraged by this assessment; Jesus provides some insights into how to become more spiritual in the following passage:

*Make a tree good and its fruit will be good, or make a tree bad and its fruit will be bad, for a tree is recognized by its fruit. You brood of vipers, how can you who are evil say anything good? For out of the overflow of the heart, the mouth speaks. The good man brings good*

*things out of the good stored up in him, and the evil man brings evil things out of the evil stored up in him.*
Matthew 12:33-35

To be made good, a tree requires a lot of attention and help. With ample soil, fertilizer, sunshine and water, the tree grows strong. The same process works for a heart; to become more spiritual, a heart requires motivation, information, application and inspiration. The combination of these qualities will lead to transformation. The example of the good tree in Matthew 12 gives me a great deal of hope for change. Jesus says that once the tree is good, the fruit will be good. The bottom line is: Jesus believes that our hearts, regardless of how unspiritual they are in this moment, can change. Once the change occurs, it will be obvious to all who observe the fruit. If your heart is in a bad place now, it can heal and be cleansed. Not just cleansed of sin, but it can also be cleansed of resentment, bitterness, guilt, shame, and a host of other negative emotions. We cannot bear good fruit with a heart that is full of negative emotions.

Jesus makes the point that a bad tree can be made good. An unspiritual heart can be made spiritual. We see this process occur many times in the Bible. Saul, who later became Paul, is a great example of someone who became more spiritual. His spirituality as a Pharisee was defined by doing. He was consumed by activity and was the poster boy for "doing." Even after becoming a Christian, he was a "doer." If it were not for his time in prison, we would probably never have his writings and a large part of the New Testament. His time in prison allowed him time to slow down, write and participate in the activities that made him reflect upon his relationship with God. In order to become more spiritual and to have spiritual breakthroughs, you will also need time for introspection, reflection, evaluation and meditation.

The Pharisees were "doers." Much of their "doing" led to hypocrisy, and so did mine. Do not fall into the trap that the more you do, the more spiritual you are. This deceitful, works-oriented path will keep you from dealing with your heart. The more in motion I was, the less I had to deal with me. I was in motion doing religious things but going through the motions spiritually. There is a balance between "doing" things like serving others and "being" a servant. The motive behind the service is the important thing. Are you serving others to work your way to heaven? Are you serving and saying yes to requests because you are afraid to say no? Are you serving to please God or to please people?

Are you so busy "doing" that you aren't "dealing?" What I mean is; are you so busy helping others that you are not addressing your own issues? Some believers, particularly those in leadership positions, can become very wrapped up in good works for others, so they do not have time to deal with themselves. I was caught up in this approach for years. As a minister for 16 years, I was much more concerned about helping others than I was about dealing with myself. Titles can give us a false sense of spirituality as well. The scary thing was that I was not even aware of what was happening to me as I was helping others. Many leaders are not aware of this dynamic, either. Although not intentional, my busyness kept me from dealing with the issues in my own heart that were preventing further spiritual growth. Are you "doing" your activities to be more like Jesus? If the answer is yes, then you will become more like Jesus. His spiritual qualities will take over your life, and the changes will be evident. The only way to know your motive for sure is take time to be honest with yourself. If you discover that your motivation is out of balance, take some time to be honest with a friend who can help. If serving and doing other spiritual activities have lost the joy they used to bring, chances are you are hiding out in activity. Busyness can only bring joy for so long. Becoming like Jesus brings a joy that will last.

## Spirituality Starts with Humility

Jesus' teachings centered on spiritual qualities from the very beginning of His ministry. His sermon recorded early in the book of Matthew is mostly about the spiritual qualities it takes to enter the Kingdom. What scholars call the "Sermon on the Mount" is really the "Sermon on the Heart." Jesus took this opportunity to transfer His heart to His listeners. Look at how Jesus begins His Sermon on the Heart. "Blessed are the poor in spirit, for theirs is the kingdom of heaven" (Matthew 5:3). Jesus begins with the spiritual quality of humility. Without humility, we cannot learn to be like Jesus. We need humility to stop making excuses and start taking responsibility for our actions, which paves the way for positive change. Humility works out difficulties with others, offers grace, extends mercy, and forgives others and ourselves. Humility teaches us how to think like Jesus and share His heart for serving others. Sharing in the character and humility of Jesus opens the door to a more intimate relationship with God.

Jesus made it very clear from the beginning of His ministry that His Kingdom was not earthly but spiritual. His disciples had a difficult time grasping the concept that Jesus wanted His followers to be spiritual. His life was dedicated to growing spiritually and spreading the news of a spiritual kingdom. God does not just want His children to be saved, but He also wants them to be spiritual. If you are a child of God, you must ask yourself if you want what God wants for you. God's Kingdom cannot be spiritual if the members of that Kingdom are not spiritual. If you are a part of His Kingdom, Jesus expects you to become more spiritual. Following His life and His teachings will guide you. Are you willing to change in order to be the person God is calling you to be? If so, start praying for the humility you will need to make the spiritual breakthroughs you seek.

The beginning of Jesus' sermon is what we call the "Beatitudes," because these qualities describe what our *attitudes* should *be*. Jesus could have started His sermon with any quality He wanted but chose humility. Jesus practiced this spiritual quality throughout His life. He even practiced humility regarding the type of death God chose for Him: "And being found in appearance as a man, he humbled himself and became obedient to death—even death on a cross!" (Philippians 2:8). Transformation into the image of Christ begins and ends with humility. It takes humility to continue the transformation process, especially when we fail. Humility teaches us to fail forward. Humility will teach us that failure is not fatal, and the only true failure is not trying. Humility will keep us focused on God and not ourselves. Humility will confront our entitlement, help us accept life on God's terms and not our own, and guide us to lead more selfless and obedient lives.

You have demonstrated some humility thus far in the transformation process by seeking help through this book. Your humility will be tested when you are called to seek help from others. My prayer is that you continue to grow in the spiritual quality of humility.

**Spirituality Ends with Pride**

Pride puts the brakes on breakthroughs. I am very familiar with this opposing quality of humility that the Bible refers to as pride:

*Pride goes before destruction,*
*   a haughty spirit before a fall.*

*Better to be lowly in spirit and among the oppressed*
*than to share plunder with the proud.*
Proverbs 16:18-19

Pride leads us to live life our way rather than God's way. Pride makes us self-reliant rather than God-dependent. Pride does not lead us to be poor in spirit or hunger and thirst for righteousness. Pride leads us to be a problem maker, not a peacemaker, producing the opposite of all of the spiritual qualities that Jesus taught and bringing the whole spiritual growth process to a grinding halt. We cannot make breakthroughs being prideful. For several years, I was the poster boy for pride. I now understand that I am never more like Jesus than when I am humble. I also understand that rebellion to God is based in pride. It was a sobering moment when I realized that I am never more like Satan than when I am prideful.

Part of my reasoning for holding on to pride was that I didn't understand what it means to be humble. I confused humility with humiliation and other negative worldly concepts. Gaining a better understanding of humility helped me pursue this spiritual quality more. Humility is misunderstood for various reasons, including a distinct lack of role models exuding this quality. It is not a quality the world honors or highlights. Another reason for the misunderstanding of the word humility is that some Bible translations use the word "meek" for "humble." I, like many other believers, assumed that meek means weak. I was never so wrong. There is nothing weak about humility.

## Humility in Action

The Bible calls Moses the most humble man of his time (Numbers 12:3). A weak man could not have rallied a nation of discouraged slaves to follow God's command to leave Egypt. A weak man would not have confronted Pharaoh, the most powerful ruler in the world at that time, on multiple occasions about his pride. A weak man could not have opposed the whole Israelite nation on their idolatry, forcing them to grind up the golden calf they made, pour it in water, and drink it. A weak man could not have led the Israelites for 40 years in the desert to the brink of the Promised Land. Only a man who was God-reliant could have done such things. Moses was far from weak, but he was humble.

Paul said he served the Lord with great humility and tears (Acts 20:19). Paul was also far from weak, traveling on at least three missionary journeys and venturing thousands of miles to plant so many churches. A weak man could neither have led hundreds of people to Christ nor helped their nascent churches grow and prosper. A weak man could not have endured imprisonments, floggings, beatings, shipwrecks and a host of other trials. He could not have encouraged followers from different races, cultures and religious backgrounds to unite for the cause of Christ. Paul was not a weak man, but he was humble.

Jesus described himself in Matthew 11:29 as humble and gentle in heart. A weak man could not have fasted for 40 days and nights or cleared the temple, as He did in Jerusalem, with whips. A weak man could not have confronted the religious leaders of the day at the risk of his life or endured the cross and all that led up to the Passion. Jesus was not a weak man, but He was a humble man.

I hope by now you get the point that took me years to understand. Humility is not a lack of strength. Humility is strength under control. It is surrendering our God-given strengths to the One who gave them to us in the first place. Humble people allow God to use them for His purposes. Humility is not the absence of pride but is the opposite of pride. These two qualities will co-exist in the same heart.

Moses and Paul had their "pride attacks," but the overall virtue in their life was humility. They did not view themselves as better than others but viewed themselves with sober judgment. Humility led them to change and be used mightily by God. Becoming more humble will lead you to breakthroughs you never dreamed of. You get to choose how humble you will be.

## Becoming More Humble

So, how do we become more humble, you ask? My experience is that humility can be acquired in only two ways. We can humble ourselves, or God will humble us; the choice is ours. God desperately wants us to have this spiritual quality, so we can make it to heaven. If we choose not to be humble, He will ensure that we get the opportunity to acquire the humility we need. Jesus humbled Himself and came to Earth to show us what true humility looks like. He came to lead a spiritual Kingdom of followers with this quality. Take this opportunity to become more humble. For years I was confused and therefore very uncomfortable with the concept of humility. If you have similar emotions, I hope you push through them and pursue humility, so you can make the spiritual breakthroughs you desire.

There are many examples of people humbling themselves before God in the Bible. Several good examples occur in the Old Testament. The vile king Ahab humbled himself with fasting, tearing his clothes, and wearing sackcloth (I Kings 21). King Josiah humbled himself with weeping, tore his robes, and inquired of the Lord (2 Kings 22). In both situations, God responded to the people humbling themselves by sparing them some type of disaster. Unlike these kings, there were times that I did not listen to God or others, and disaster struck. After experiencing several such disasters, I learned that humbling myself is the better way. Humbling ourselves is difficult, but I have found that having God humble me is even more painful.

God has humbled me in the past, and it is not pleasant. My pride showed up at church, on the job, in my marriage, in my parenting, and at sporting events; it did not discriminate. My pride was with me wherever I went. I could not leave it at the door. I would do and say things to embarrass myself, my wife, and my children. It caused me to be argumentative, resistant, and defensive, and to make foolish decisions. I therefore tarnished my reputation and my integrity by doing things my way. I made poor financial choices with dire consequences because I did not seek advice from others who were very qualified to help. I am convinced that pride is in every molecule of my DNA. That is why I must address it every day. My pride takes no holidays.

I have learned from personal experience and the testimony of many Biblical examples that resisting God is stupid. I rarely use that word, but look at these examples. Pharaoh's pride led to his destruction. In spite of God's mighty hand demonstrated through the ten plagues upon his people, Pharaoh would not relent to God. His pride drove him to continue to resist God. This prideful approach led to the destruction of his country, the death of his first-born, and the loss of his own life. Pride makes us do stupid things. Resisting the creator of the universe is stupid, no matter who you are or what you think you have accomplished. Take some time and reflect to see if there are ways you are resisting God.

In Daniel 4, the Bible tells the story of King Nebuchadnezzar who built the great kingdom of Babylon for himself. The king did not give God the credit for this accomplishment in spite of contrary warnings from the prophet Daniel. The end result of the king's pride was that he went from feasting on gourmet dishes to dining on grass with the cattle. The king went from riches to rags, from palace to pasture. He finally acknowledged God, and his sanity was restored.

The Apostle Peter experienced what it was like to be humbled. He and the other apostles, at times, argued about who was going to be first in this new and spiritual Kingdom Jesus proclaimed. Obviously, Peter missed the point of the humility necessary to enter this Kingdom. One such occasion occurred in Mark 9. Jesus confronted His apostles, arguing over who would be the greatest, and they all got quiet. Jesus told them if they want to be first, they must be last; and they must become more like a child to be greatest. Jesus showed them that humility was the way to greatness. It is humbling to be called out on our sin and shown up by a kid, especially in front of others. In Luke 22, the apostles are humbled once again. The night before He died, Jesus predicted they would all fall away on account of Him. All of the disciples adamantly disagreed, but each deserted Jesus later that night. In their pride, they relied upon their own strength and best thinking, and they were humbled by failure. The pain of our failures due to self-reliance can lead us to be haughty or humble. I now choose the road of humility.

There are many other Biblical examples of people being humbled by God and people humbling themselves. I shared these few examples, so we get the point that God wants us to be humble. God humbles all of us at times. Every time I took over the controls of my life, I crashed and burned, and God humbled me. He allowed me to suffer the consequences of living life my way, so I could learn how to live life His way. The consequences were painful but saved my life. These experiences radically changed my life because I decided that I never want to feel the depth of that type of pain again. The depth of the emotional pain of being humbled by God is difficult to describe but an experience that I will never forget. Resisting God's call to greater spiritual growth will only result in pain and negative consequences. Thankfully, God is gracious, and He allows us to eventually get our act together and get humble. If you choose the path of humility now, you will spare yourself more pain. If you do not choose the humble path, you will suffer more. God gives us the choice. The apostles humbled out and became great men. God wants to lead you to become more like His Son, but He cannot do that without humility.

## Trained not Tortured

Peter failed many times due to pride. As he became more humble, he learned to allow his failures to make him a more spiritual man. Peter learned how to let his failures train and transform him rather than to torture him. Many of God's children are tortured on a daily basis for their worldly, cowardly and sinful decisions of the past that were based in pride. Imagine how Peter must have tortured himself for his failures up to the resurrection. Look at what Peter had to say about pride and humility:

*"God opposes the proud but gives grace to the humble." Humble your-selves, therefore, under God's mighty hand, that he may lift you up in due time. Cast all your anxiety on him because he cares for you.*
I Peter 5:5b-7

If the apostle Peter can make breakthroughs to con-quer his pride and become a more spiritual man, so can we. Pride causes us to ask ourselves, "How could I have been so stupid?" Yet beating ourselves up, putting our-selves down, and constantly filling our minds with nega-tive thoughts about ourselves are not examples of humility. These approaches are self-destructive and will also lead to disaster. To overcome poor choices of the past, we must humble ourselves enough to get the help we need to grow from these experiences. Your failures and the resulting consequences can be the very thing you need to get to heaven. In a spiritual kingdom, we must have a spiritual approach to addressing our failures and weaknesses.

To conclude this discussion on pride and humility, understand that both are a choice. Jesus *always* chose humility, and so can we. This choice may be very difficult to make, but we still get to choose. This notion of choice is very empowering for me. I previously believed that I was programmed for pride and destined to reap its consequences, but I now perceive this situation very differently. If we follow Jesus, He will teach us how to be humble, even in difficult situations.

**Chapter 4**

# The Spirit

## The Role of the Spirit

In order to become more spiritual, it makes sense that we must have a better understanding of the Holy Spirit. One of the roles of the Spirit's work is to help us become more spiritual. The Spirit of God is introduced in the first verse of the Bible and has been active ever since, from creation to the present. The following verses are from the writings of Paul, provided to deepen your convictions; Christians have the Spirit, and the Spirit wants to work in the life of those who possess this amazing gift.

*And hope does not disappoint us, because God has poured out his love into our hearts by the Holy Spirit, whom he has given us.*
Romans 5:5

*Don't you know that you yourselves are God's temple and that God's Spirit lives in you?*
I Corinthians 3:16

*Now it is God who makes both us and you stand firm in Christ. He anointed us, set his seal of ownership on us, and put his Spirit in our hearts as a deposit, guaranteeing what is to come.*
2 Corinthians 1:21-22

*May He grant you out of the rich treasury of His glory to be strength-ened and reinforced with mighty power in the inner man by the [Holy] Spirit [Himself indwelling your innermost being and personality].*
Ephesians 3:16, AMP

*Through the power of the Holy Spirit who lives within us, carefully guard the precious truth that has been entrusted to you.*
2 Timothy 1:14, NLT

My personal favorite scripture about the Spirit living within us is from Romans 8.

*And if the Spirit of him who raised Jesus from the dead is living in you, he who raised Christ from the dead will also give life to your mortal bodies through his Spirit, who lives in you.*
Romans 8:11

Notice how personally Paul describes the Spirit. Paul asserts that the power which caused the resurrection of Jesus from the dead resides in each Christian. Due to advanced medical technology, we are familiar with people being "brought back to life." In spite of modern medicine, no one in this day and age is brought back to life after three whole days. Jesus arose, not to give us spiritual existence, but spiritual excellence. He was brought back to life to give us freedom from the things that enslave us. Jesus' victory over the grave was both physical and spiritual. Due to the resurrection of Jesus from the dead, we can change. The Spirit living within us will enable us to make and sustain *any* spiritual breakthrough we desire.

Paul explains the role of the Spirit in a Christian life. The Bible says we are to "live by the Spirit" (Galatians 5:16), implying that spirituality is a 24/7 lifestyle. This concept was difficult for me to grasp. In order to grow spirituality, I realized I had to live by the Spirit *all* the time. I am now convinced that I can live by the Spirit *all* the time because the Spirit lives in me *all* the time. The Spirit does not come and go. I do not wake up in the morning and wonder, "Do I have the Spirit?" The Spirit does not leave us even when we sleep. It is with us constantly. The question is, "Will I allow the Spirit to work in me on a continual basis or only when I feel like it?" When I allow the Spirit to work, I am victorious over sin and can make any spiritual breakthrough I desire.

The Bible says, "Since we live by the Spirit, let us keep in step with the Spirit" (Galatians 5:25). When I was in the Army, we often marched together as a unit to go places. As we marched, someone called a cadence to keep us in step. It went something like, "left, left, left right left." This cadence is not creative, but it is effective. The joy of marching in formation cannot be put into words. As annoying as this cadence could be, it kept everyone in step. It was obvious to everyone in formation when someone was out of step because others could see it. Conversely, it is not always obvious to others that we are out of step with the Spirit, but we know it. There have been times the Spirit within me was calling a cadence I was not following. I was literally marching to the beat of a different drummer. To live by the Spirit means allowing the Spirit to control us. In the past, I did not make much progress spiritually because I was constantly going back and forth, alternately living for myself and attempting to live by the Spirit. You know from your own experience that this approach doesn't work.

Paul stated in his letter to the Philippians that we can have "fellowship with the Spirit" (Philippians 2:1). In other words, an ongoing, growing and dynamic relationship with the Spirit is possible. Fellowship implies relationship and partnership. In this relationship, the Spirit's role is to guide us. However, the Spirit cannot guide us if we do not allow it. I have often resisted the Spirit's attempts to work in my life. Paul's fellowship with the Spirit allowed him to make amazing changes; for Paul, the Spirit was real and vibrant. Is the Spirit the same for you? How is your fellowship with the Spirit going? If you are like me, you may need lots of help in getting to know the Spirit. Once I obtained a better understanding of the Spirit's role, I was more willing to let the Spirit guide me.

As in any relationship, there are things we can do to damage our relationship with the Spirit. One of Paul's final admonishments, as he closed his first letter to the church at Thessalonica, was: "Do not quench the Spirit" (1 Thessalonians 5:19). Quench means to suppress the work of the Spirit. There are several ways I can hinder the Spirit's ability to work in me. Things like willful and un-confessed sin, wrong priorities, apathy, and hopelessness for change are but a few. In what ways do you squelch the Spirit's fire? One especially stubborn way to quench the Spirit is to ignore it. In other words, there were times when I made a conscience decision not to let the Spirit lead me. In the past, I have heard the Spirit calling me to go in one direction, yet I went in another. In these situations, I made a decision to sin and go against the wishes of the Father, the Son, and the Holy Spirit. Making this decision on a consistent basis results in a different lifestyle than what God intends for his children. In the past, I claimed to be a Son of God but acted like a slave to sin.

## Spiritual Drag Queen

The religious world has a term for people who proclaim a lifestyle of one thing yet live out another — hypocrites.

You know some. You may even be one. This book will help you make the spiritual breakthroughs you need in order to overcome your charade. The word hypocrite comes from the ancient Greek theater and means "play-acting." The psychological world has a word for those who play-act a different gender. These individuals are called transvestites. Let me explain.

As a Christian I am supposed to be clothed with Christ, as Paul told the Christians at various churches:

*Rather, clothe yourselves with the Lord Jesus Christ, and do not think about how to gratify the desires of the sinful nature.*
Romans 13:14

*You are all sons of God through faith in Christ Jesus, for all of you who were baptized into Christ have clothed yourselves with Christ.*
Galatians 3:26-27

*Therefore, as God's chosen people, holy and dearly loved, clothe yourselves with compassion, kindness, humility, gentleness and patience.*
Colossians 3:12

When I am clothed with Jesus, people will notice. When I am wrapped up in myself, I am overdressed. Fashion tells a lot about the person. The problem I had in the past was that I could change my spiritual clothes faster than a runway model or a fire fighter. The slang term for someone who dresses in clothes that are not in accordance with their gender is called a "drag queen." These are usually men who dress in women's clothes, completing the ensemble with feminine makeup and mannerisms. Some transvestites are so skilled at dressing and acting like a woman, you cannot tell the difference. Drag queens take on the qualities of feminism for brief periods of time then return to looking and acting like a man again.

Many people of faith find the lifestyle of a transvestite to be disagreeable. However, in the past, I took this same approach, metaphorically speaking, to my spirituality, and perhaps, you have too. There were times in my Christian life that I was a Christian *most* of the time. However, there were other times when I dressed and acted like the world and later changed back into my Christian clothes. I grew convicted that I was behaving like a spiritual drag queen, dressing up like the world, acting like the world, but returning to my Christian state. Putting my actions into the context of this lifestyle helped me gain a stronger conviction about making a spiritual breakthrough in this area.

I decided that being a spiritual transvestite is no way to live. Perhaps you can relate. The lifestyle is confusing and demoralizing. I can't recall a time when I went back to the world briefly and felt good about my relationship with God or myself afterwards. So I decided to add to my spiritual wardrobe and throw out the clothes of this world. I have never regretted that decision. You cannot make spiritual breakthroughs jumping back and forth from the world to the Spirit. You must commit to one or the other. That's why, in the book of Revelations, Jesus told the church at Laodicea to be hot or cold.

*I know your deeds, that you are neither cold nor hot. I wish you were either one or the other! So, because you are lukewarm—neither hot nor cold—I am about to spit you out of my mouth.*
Revelations 3:15-16

I choose to be hot, on fire with the Spirit, and continually do what it takes to stay hot. You can do the same, but you may need to achieve spiritual breakthroughs in the areas that are holding you back and work through your fears in order for you to get hot and stay hot. You must believe you have what it takes. This book will help you find a way to make and sustain the changes you want to make. It will help you see the amazing power of God and the Holy Spirit, discover how to be strengthened by the body of Christ, and realize your own strengths as well.

## Spiritual Qualities

When we live by the Spirit and are led by the Spirit, we will grow spiritually and demonstrate various qualities of the Spirit. There are several meaty sections of the New Testament perfectly suited for a study on spirituality. Matthew 5-7, Romans 8 and 12, Galatians 5, 2 Peter 1 and others present a great deal of spiritual qualities. From these sections, I developed a list of spiritual traits. Jesus exemplified all of these qualities and more, expecting His followers to strive for the same. The Holy Spirit will help us to increasingly embody each of these qualities if we are willing.

Paul told the church in Ephesus, "Do not get drunk on wine, which leads to debauchery. Instead, be filled with the Spirit" (Ephesians 5:18). I am not exactly sure what "filled with the Spirit" means, but it sounds awesome. In the past I was filled with pride, lust, selfishness, alcohol, and a host of other worldly things. The times I was led by unspiritual qualities resulted in great regret. However, I have never regretted my decision and efforts to become more spiritual.

I've compiled a list of qualities to help you visualize what spirituality looks like. If this list seems overwhelming, do not panic. Remember, spirituality is a process. These are traits you pursue for a lifetime. Each baby step of progress in any of these traits gets you closer to the person you want to be. My goal each day is to end the day more like Jesus than when I started. Each day affords plenty of opportunities to work on many of these traits. In my journey of transformation into the likeness of Christ, I have experienced breakthroughs in many of these areas. Needless to say, I need to make countless more. Now, I consider the process of making more breakthroughs an exciting one, rather than the excruciating experience I had perceived in the past. My mindset about the process improved because I have reaped the rewards of the changes I made. I am nowhere near my goal in pursuit of these Jesus-like qualities, but I am a lot closer than I used to be.

| | | |
|---|---|---|
| Compassion | Gratitude | Purity |
| Conviction | Hope | Righteousness |
| Devotion | Humility | Sacrificing |
| Discipline | Joy | Self-Denial |
| Faith | Kindness | Sensitivity |
| Forgiveness | Love | Submission |
| Generosity | Loyalty | Trust |
| Gentleness | Passion | Truth |
| Godliness | Patience | Understanding |
| Grace | Peace | Wisdom |

Most of the Christian clients I work with set goals to become "more spiritual." So I ask, "What does that look like to you?" They often have a difficult time defining this goal. I find that many Christians can name few qualities of the Spirit. They just know they want to do better in a particular area of their life, like controlling their thoughts, managing their emotions or changing a behavior. These believers deduce that progress in one of these areas will make them more spiritual. This line of thinking is logical but not necessarily true. These Christians want to become more spiritual by stopping something worldly without necessarily starting something spiritual. I find that most Christians pursuing breakthroughs focus on what they want to stop and not on a specific spiritual quality they want to start. These individuals attempt to change behaviors but often neglect changing who they are. In the past I was able to stop a way of worldly thinking and behaving only to replace it with another worldly thought process or practice. In order to become more spiritual, I must change not just what I do but who I am.

Changing who I am will translate into changes of how I think, how I feel, what I do, and what I pursue. If I am trying to change an addiction, for example, but do not change the person that I am, I will most likely just switch to another addiction inadvertently. The selfishness of the addiction will likely be channeled in another direction. This new direction may be less destructive, but selfishness is destructive in any form. Jesus said it best when He told the Pharisees to first clean the inside of the cup, then the outside will be clean. In layman's terms, spirituality is an inside job.

God's grace empowers us to manifest more of these spiritual traits by forgiving us when we fall short in our efforts to change. This list is not meant to be exhaustive but will give you specific characteristics to address in your life. A breakthrough in any of the above spiritual qualities can lead to growth in other areas of your life. I encourage you to pick one or two of these traits that you really want to change. Define the term, find Biblical examples of God, Jesus, or others demonstrating the trait, and start working on it. It is important to start somewhere. Reading the rest of this book will equip you to better embrace more of any of these virtues.

The most important quality for you to possess at this point is willingness to be more spiritual. Change will not occur if we are not willing and don't allow it to happen. Our lack of willingness to change at the present time may be due to discouragement. Many Christians have repeatedly tried to change one or more of these traits in the past and failed. Perhaps due to ignorance about one or more of these qualities, you may be holding on to the worldly opposite of a spiritual trait; for example, I held onto pride, mistakenly equating humility with weakness. I could not embrace sacrifice as long as I held on to the worldly characteristics of greed and selfishness. A deeper understanding of these spiritual qualities led me to desire to grow more in each trait.

I continue to work on each of these spiritual qualities daily. I also struggle against each opposing worldly trait on a daily basis. We are in a spiritual battle for each of these virtues, and I have experienced the thrill of victory and the agony of defeat for each of them. However, I continue to desire more of each attribute because Jesus possessed each of them. Some I am more eager to change than others, and some are more difficult than others. However, I am committed to change and striving to be more of each of these traits. Your commitment to change will lead you to a more fulfilling and spiritual life as well.

Chapter 5

# The Foundation for Breakthroughs

### Breakthrough Defined

Now that you have a better understanding of "spiritual," we will examine the second part of the term "spiritual breakthrough." What exactly is a "breakthrough?" The Merriam-Webster online dictionary defines a breakthrough as "a significant or sudden advance, development, achievement or increase that removes a barrier to progress." You will not find the term "spiritual breakthrough" in the dictionary, the Bible, or in many other books. You may have never heard the term before, which tells us how rare they can be. If more people were making spiritual breakthroughs, more people would be talking about them. A spiritual breakthrough is more than just changing something about yourself. Making and sustaining spiritual breakthroughs will transform you into a radically different person. As a result of this metamorphosis, you will be increasingly like Jesus. That is what the power of God can do if we allow it.

As I mentioned, making changes is different than a making a breakthrough. Have you ever changed something and no one noticed? By definition, that is not a breakthrough. The Apostle Peter is a great example of someone who made and sustained spiritual breakthroughs. In John 1:42, Jesus first meets Simon and nicknames him Peter. The Greek word used here for Peter is *petros*, which means a rock like a small stone or pebble. The night preceding the crucifixion, Peter was truly a pebble. Out of fear, Peter the Pebble ran away from the mob that came to arrest Jesus. That same night, he denied Jesus three times when confronted by a servant girl. Due to fear, Peter the Pebble was not at the cross when Jesus was crucified. As a result of discouragement, he was not present at the resurrection of Jesus. Pebble Peter, like many current-day disciples of Jesus, experienced intense negative emotions and did not address them in a very spiritual manner.

However, in the book of Acts, Peter the Pebble is transformed, becoming a different man and making amazing spiritual breakthroughs in addressing his emotions. In Galatians 2:9, Paul refers to Peter as a pillar of the church. In Acts 2, Peter the Pillar preaches a sermon God used to save 3,000 people just 50 days after the crucifixion. The Pillar boldly faces persecution in Acts 4 when he tells the religious leaders that he obeys God rather than man, and the Bible says they noted the courage of Peter. In Acts 10, Peter is used to usher the Gentiles into the church. He boldly faces imprisonment and even death in Acts 12. As a result of making spiritual breakthroughs in fear and discouragement, Peter goes from a pebble to a pillar of the early church. Peter's more spiritual approach to dealing with his emotions led to his transformation.

The Bible provides many examples of others who made and sustained spiritual breakthroughs. Saul became the Apostle Paul. John, who Jesus nicknamed the "Son of

Thunder," later became the "Apostle of Love." The men and women who radically changed in the Bible can inspire you and give you hope; this radical transformation can happen to you as well. Your example of making spiritual breakthroughs can also inspire others to do the same.

## Choosing the Right Foundation

The proper foundation is *absolutely crucial* to making and sustaining spiritual breakthroughs. Many Christians fail at attempts to change because they lack the proper foundation. Their efforts are often based upon feelings. For example, they may initially feel excited about working on some aspect of their life, like going on a diet to lose extra holiday pounds. But as time goes on, the feelings may change due to discouragement from a lack of progress. Since the initial decision to go on a diet was based on emotions, the decision to stop was easy because the emotions changed. In other words, they gave in to their feelings. It is easy to allow emotions to dictate the decisions we make to change. This approach to change did not work well for me. The foundation for making breakthroughs *must* consist of more than just emotions.

Many believers fail to make and sustain spiritual breakthroughs because they lack a *spiritual* foundation. They attempt to change something based on an *unspiritual* foundation, like emotions. Their attempts to change are built on sand rather than rock. I do not remember much about Sunday school classes, but I do remember some of the songs. One of my favorites as a kid was "The Wise Man Built His House on the Rock." I bet the song is playing in your head right now, and you probably even remember the hand motions. The song is based on the following teaching of Jesus:

*Therefore everyone who hears these words of mine and puts them into practice is like a wise man who built his house on the rock. The rain came down, the streams rose, and the winds blew and beat against that house; yet it did not fall, because it had its foundation on the rock. But everyone who hears these words of mine and does not put them into practice is like a foolish man who built his house on sand. The rain came down, the streams rose, and the winds blew and beat against that house, and it fell with a great crash.*
Matthew 7:24-27

Every difficult situation we experience is an opportunity for a breakthrough or a breakdown; the choice is ours. I experienced many breakdowns because my attempts to change were based upon emotions. The end result of these attempts was failure and a great deal of anger, frustration and ultimately, hopelessness. For years I broke down because I did not *feel* like I could handle my problems in a spiritual manner. I regularly gave in to my emotions about these failures and used worldly methods to manage my difficult emotions. This process resulted in becoming a slave to my emotions. My feelings became the wind that dictated my behaviors. These winds blew me to do all kinds of things that I did not want to do — even things I hated. I learned I cannot control the wind, but I can learn to adjust the sails.

In order to make and sustain spiritual breakthroughs, we must not just b*elieve* the Bible. We must have a *conviction* about the Bible. There is a difference between a belief and a conviction. A belief is something I hold on to. A conviction holds on to me. Not only do we need to believe the Bible, but we also need to have deep convictions about it. A conviction is a fixed or firm belief. The early disciples radically changed so much due to their deep convictions about the Scriptures. Paul shared these words with the church in Thessalonica, "because our gospel came to you not simply with words, but also with power, with the Holy Spirit and with deep conviction" (I Thessalonians 1:5). Convictions are important because, as we go through the breakthrough process, we will experience a host of negative emotions like fear, doubt, insecurity, discouragement, anxiety and others. In order to combat these emotions, we need to have a deep trust in God that His power and His Spirit will guide us through them.

I now have the conviction that wherever God's will takes me, His grace will sustain me. I have the conviction that where God guides, He will provide. These convictions about God's promises now guide me through the storms of life rather than my feelings. You will need not only spiritual beliefs but also convictions based upon the right foundation. The Bible is that foundation of rock because it does not change. The Bible uses a different word for rock in the above verses. The word used is *petra* which means boulder or cliff. During a recent visit to the Grand Canyon with my wife, we learned some of the rocks there are *two billion* years old. I am sure you are not rushing to make plans to go see these rocks before they disappear. These rocks will be there long after we are gone. They have endured countless storms and will endure countless more. A life built upon the Rock will endure the storms of life; building your life on the Bible will give you the convictions you need to weather any storm.

Emotions, on the other hand, are quite the opposite. Our emotions and moods are affected by almost anything. Building a life on emotions is like building a house on sand. Unlike rocks, storms have a huge impact on sand; almost anything moves sand. If you watch waves come to shore, you can see them carry sand in and out. Little children move sand to make castles, and crabs move sand to dig holes. Waves, crabs and babies do not move the type of rocks described in the above teaching of Jesus. Many great crashes and breakdowns are afflicting too many Christians due to a poor spiritual foundation. Their lives are built on sand and not the unshakeable stability of boulders.

Christians can go through many types of dangerous storms: the death of a loved one, divorce, an addiction, a mental illness, bankruptcy, a chronic disease and many more. Sometimes we are hit with more than one storm at a time. Weathering storms in a house built upon sand can be devastating. It can take years to rebuild after such storms, and sadly, many decide to rebuild on sand. Now is a good time to decide to build your life on the Rock. In practical terms, this means stop basing your decisions to change on how *you* feel, and base them on how *God* feels. You will see a huge difference in the outcome. As we go through the breakthrough process, our feelings will tell us to stop when the pain starts. Our convictions can lead us through the pain to the gains we seek. The Biblical examples I use to demonstrate how to make spiritual breakthroughs throughout the book all illustrate this approach.

## The Bible is the Word of God

*All Scripture is God-breathed and is useful for teaching, rebuking, correcting and training in righteousness, so that the man of God may be thoroughly equipped for every good work.*
2 Timothy 3:16-17

In order to make spiritual breakthroughs, you will need to accept the basic spiritual principle that the Bible is the inspired Word of God. The Bible is the Rock upon which we must base our lives. Why is this so important? The Bible will provide you the truth about you, the life that you are living, and the life you can live. All of the excuses we can make for lack of change must be confronted with truth. All of our rationalizations to stay the same must be brought into the light. We must believe the truth of God over our feelings and even our best thinking. Jesus stated in John 14:6, "I am the way and the truth and the life." We must believe God is showing us the way to live through His Son, His Spirit and His Word.

When we trust God, His Word will empower us to have victories we never imagined. Doubting God's truth will result in failure. Satan tempted Adam and Eve to doubt God, and they failed miserably. Satan merely asked them, "Did God really say…?" Expect Satan to use the same approach with us. One of Satan's best schemes is to create doubt. I fell for this scheme many times and had to learn that doubt results in spiritual breakdowns. We will be tempted to doubt the promises of God such as: "I can do everything through Christ," (Philippians 4:13, NLT) and, "we are more than conquerors" (Romans 8:37). Too many times in my Christian life, I believed my doubts and doubted my beliefs. I repeatedly succumbed to the schemes of Satan. But I changed my approach, and the outcome changed. I decided to believe God's word over my doubts and fears. I decided to run on conviction and not emotion. Once we get the spiritual convictions we need, Jesus promised that nothing will be impossible for us (Luke 1:37).

There are plenty of fine secular books written by knowledgeable people who can help us with the changes we desire. I have read many such books and learned a great deal from them. This book, however, is based on the premise that the Bible is *the* instruction manual for life. You may remember the old saying, "When all else fails, read the instructions." In the past and on multiple occasions, I have attempted to assemble something without first consulting the instructions. As my wife can attest, this "guy approach" of charging into assembling something without reading the instructions does not work well. She has seen me take this approach with everything from gas grills to baby cribs. She also saw me take this same approach to my spiritual life. An attempt to live life without consulting God's instructions is an exercise in futility. This approach leads to frustration and failure. God's approach leads to success. By this time in your life, maybe all else has failed, and it is time to get back to the instruction manual. It is time to get back to the Being who knit you together in your mother's womb and the Book that He wrote to teach us how to live. It's time to believe that you can and will be successful in making the breakthroughs you desire.

## Jesus is our Example to Follow

In order to make spiritual breakthroughs, it is essential to get back to the basics of Christianity. One of these important basics was discussed earlier in the chapter: believing the Bible over our feelings. Following the example of Jesus is another essential key to making and sustaining spiritual breakthroughs. Many Christians are caught up in the dictionary definition of Christianity versus the *Biblical* definition. The dictionary definition focuses on *believing* in Christ. God's expectations for Christians go way beyond belief. James told his readers that even the demons believe in God and shudder (James 2:19). Many Christians stumble into the sin that so easily entangles because they stop following the example of Jesus. God's goal for His children is transformation into the likeness of Christ.

*Now the Lord is the Spirit, and where the Spirit of the Lord is, there is freedom. And we, who with unveiled faces all reflect the Lord's glory, are being transformed into his likeness with ever-increasing glory, which comes from the Lord, who is the Spirit.*
2 Corinthians 3:17-18

The truth is that we become like what we worship. If we have worldly priorities, we will be transformed into what the world has to offer. We will also suffer the consequences of that transformation. If we follow Jesus, we will be transformed into His likeness, and we will reap the rewards. This verse expresses that if we follow Jesus, we will go from one degree of glory to another. We will be freed from bondage to those things that enslave us, regardless of what they are. We will become more and more like Jesus and less and less like ourselves. The ultimate outcome is a more Christ-like version of you.

I can understand that accepting Jesus as Lord is difficult for some people. Some of my difficulties with this decision were due to a lack of understanding of Jesus. My impression of Jesus while growing up was that He spent a lot of time blessing children and talking about flowers and farm animals. The pictures of Jesus in Sunday school class were of a well-groomed, tanned man who looked more like a magazine model than a martyr. This concept of Jesus was inaccurate and uninspiring, but it stuck with me into early adulthood. This image neither inspired me to change my life nor called me to be different. Getting to know the Jesus of the Bible did both. By the time I got to meet and understand the real Jesus, I was enslaved to all sorts of sin. My life was well out of line with God's plan for me. I had to let God take over. I had to make Jesus Lord of my life. The decision was terrifying but extremely gratifying. I believe you will find the same results.

I know hundreds of Christians who have made breakthroughs, but I cannot attribute these breakthroughs to mere psychological interventions. The breakthroughs they made were based on accepting the truth of the Bible, obeying God's Word over feelings, and following the example of Jesus. If you can do these things, you are on your way to tapping into God's power and making the breakthroughs you desire. The reason so many believers continue to fail to make spiritual breakthroughs is that their emotions run their life. In order to make spiritual breakthroughs, truth must guide your life. The more you view and react to the world as Jesus did, the more spiritual you will become.

**Transformed by Truth**

In order to be transformed into the likeness of Christ, we must be immersed in the truth. Jesus was full of truth, and we must be immersed in Him. We can all relate to the statement that the truth hurts. Thankfully, Jesus was also full of grace. We need to accept and embrace the grace available to us as we come to accept the truth about ourselves.

*The Word became flesh and made his dwelling among us. We have seen his glory, the glory of the One and Only, who came from the Father, full of grace and truth.*
John 1:14

*To the Jews who had believed him, Jesus said, "If you hold to my teaching, you are really my disciples. Then you will know the truth, and the truth will set you free."*
John 8:31-32

To make the breakthroughs you desire, you will need to be armed with truth and learn to make the proper response to the truth. Many believers fail to change because they view themselves very differently than God does. They describe themselves as a loser, a failure, or some other negative term. God does not see us that way. God sees us as sinners but also as His children who are special in His eyes. The truth is that God always has a vision for us, regardless of our lack of vision for ourselves. If you are in this situation, let the truth heal your hurt heart. Let His grace do its work to get you back on the path of righteousness.

Other believers come from the opposite end of this spiritual spectrum. They barely see they have a problem at all. They have ears but do not hear and eyes but do not see. They are heavily armed with defense mechanisms in order to remain the same. They purport to be fine and assume the rest of the world has a problem. The not-so clinical term for this person is *clueless*. I was totally clueless in many areas of my life. I had a black belt in several defense mechanisms. I needed mega-doses of truth to see that I was the problem. The truth helped cut through my heart, so I could change. Grace helped me deal with all of my pain and sorrow once I let it impact my heart. Embracing God's grace will help you do the same.

### The Mirror is not a Mirage

*Do not merely listen to the word, and so deceive yourselves. Do what it says. Anyone who listens to the word but does not do what it says is like a man who looks at his face in a mirror and, after looking at himself, goes away and immediately forgets what he looks like. But the man who looks intently into the perfect law that gives freedom, and continues to do this, not forgetting what he has heard, but doing it—he will be blessed in what he does.*
James 1:22-25

The Bible is the mirror of our soul. James is making it clear that it is not what we know about the Bible but what we apply that will make the difference in our lives. There are many believers who are looking into the Bible, but they are not applying the teachings. They are like the man who looks into the mirror and forgets what he looks like. Some see the need for change but have lost hope. Others purposely forget what they see, so they do not need to deal with their lives. Some choose to forget what they see because want to forget the past. Others look into the mirror and forget because they do not want to remember who they used to be. They stopped being transformed into Jesus because they conformed to the world. They stare and wonder how they went from godly to godless. They ask, "How did this reverse transformation occur? How did one who loved God and His Word so much become so unlike Him?" Others are focused on the negative aspects of their lives, rather than the good that resides there. They have lost sight of who they are and whose they are.

Regardless of your situation, you need to go to the mirror. Not the rear view mirror of the past but God's mirror. If you are like me, you will not always like what you see. This mirror is not like some you'll find at the county fair, making you look different than you really are. God's mirror will show you the truth. Looking intently into the mirror and addressing what you see takes courage and a conscious decision. The late Michael Jackson inspired many to look at themselves through the words of his famous song "Man in the Mirror." (For a link to the music video of this song and others mentioned throughout this book, visit my web site at www.mtccounseling.com.) The point of the song is that change starts with us. I found that all of the energy I put into trying to change others and situations that I could not control was of no benefit. This approach kept the man in the mirror the same.

Many Christians are taking the same approach and are attempting to change the world without first addressing the person in the mirror. Be the change you want to see in the world. The person I was most afraid to confront was myself. Fear kept me in shame and led me to more of the same. Courage took me to new and better spiritual places. Courage is not the lack of fear but the ability to feel the fear and move forward. As you go, God will be with you. We have a courageous Savior, and we need to imitate His example as He faced His fears. Claim God's promise that if you look intently into the mirror and do the things He commands, you will be emancipated from the sin that enslaves you. Christians should be the freest people on the planet, yet many are hostages because the man in the mirror remains the same.

As Psalm 107 says,

*Some sat in darkness and the deepest gloom,*
*    prisoners suffering in iron chains,*
*for they had rebelled against the words of God*
*    and despised the counsel of the Most High.*
*So he subjected them to bitter labor;*
*    they stumbled, and there was no one to help.*
*Then they cried to the LORD in their trouble,*
*    and he saved them from their distress.*
*He brought them out of darkness and the deepest gloom*
*    and broke away their chains.*
*Let them give thanks to the LORD for his unfailing love*
*    and his wonderful deeds for men,*
*for he breaks down gates of bronze*
*    and cuts through bars of iron.*
Psalm 107:10-16

Freedom begins with crying out to God. However, you will not cry out if you do not see your situation. Some Christians are so accustomed to the dark, they have great night vision. But even with eyes wide open, there is only so much we see about ourselves in the dark. We all have spiritual blind spots. God wants to bring our darkness and spiritual blindness into the light of the Scriptures. As you know from experience, this sudden burst of light, to eyes that operated in darkness, will hurt. Your eyes, thankfully, will adjust to the light. We cannot be a light until the Light illuminates us. Fearing the Light fosters more darkness.

Now is a good time to decide to come into God's light and deal with the darkness in your life.

God wants the man in the mirror to be free from the deepest gloom, guilt and pain of the past, suffering and problems of the present, anxiety about the future, distress of constant negative thinking or an addiction, and numerous other things that can enslave His people. All of these things, however, must be brought to the Light. If you are currently in this spiritual dungeon, you are not alone. Cry out as the psalmist did and get help from God and others to gain your freedom. Independence always comes at a price. The price for me was to stop being rebellious and despising the counsel of God. Jesus won victory over death and the grave through humility and obedience. We must do the same. This is a good time to ask yourself a few but difficult questions. In what ways am I rebelling against God? What chains are holding me captive? Am I ready to cry out to God or just keep crying? What is the bitter labor that I am enduring? Do I want to trade the life I have now for a better one? Am I ready to leave my dungeon to claim my destiny? The answer to these questions will help you see if you are truly ready to make spiritual breakthroughs.

# Chapter 6

# The Approach

❧

## The Bible and Psychology

If you have ever been to therapy, you may understand the importance of knowing the approach of the therapist. Understanding the approach will help you discern if the therapist and the approach are a good fit for you and are capable of addressing your issues. I take time here to explain the therapeutic approach I use.

As you can already see, this book is not a psychology or self-help book with some vague references to the Bible. I call this a "God-help book." This is a Bible-based book that applies therapeutic tools used in the field of psychology. Some Christians have a negative view of this field of study. They often believe that all psychology has to offer is "the wisdom of this world." I agree that there is a great deal of worldliness in the field of psychology. However, the psychological interventions I use in the book work because they are based on godly principles. The Bible is not a psychology book, but there is plenty to learn about psychology from the Bible. The word psychology comes from two Greek words, *psykhe*, meaning "breath, spirit or soul," and *logia*, meaning "study of." The Bible certainly is an amazing book about the spirit and soul of mankind. From the creation of Adam and Eve, the Bible contains a wealth of information and insight into humans and how we think, feel and behave. God wants us to learn from the failures of our spiritual ancestors recorded in the Bible and imitate their successes. During the course of the book, we will read both.

The men and women I use in this book as examples of spiritual breakthroughs are from the Bible. I work with many believers in my practice who I could use as case studies to demonstrate making and sustaining spiritual breakthroughs, but I chose to use Biblical examples, providing the opportunity for you to study and imitate them. Where these individuals started in their process of change and where they ended is clearly documented in the Scriptures. You will gain a great deal of hope and inspiration from them as you read their stories.

Another aspect of my approach is sharing about my life. Paul told the Thessalonian church that he shared with them not only the gospel but his life as well. Self-disclosure is a way some therapists choose to give their clients hope and to build rapport with them. Many therapists are uncomfortable with this approach for various reasons. I think one of the things that made Jesus the "Wonderful Counselor" Isaiah describes was His openness and vulnerability. I decided a long time ago to use this method and let my past work for me by sharing it with others who are struggling with similar issues. I encourage everyone I work with to do the same. Your past will also work for you when you use it to help others.

I have made many breakthroughs since becoming a Christian. I am, by nature, extremely selfish, prideful, arrogant, and a host of other negative attributes. I am the poster child for narcissism, a very unflattering personality disorder. These qualities led me into a life of sin and self-destruction that was detrimental to me and particularly to those I love the most. Thank God for His power which gives us the ability to change our lives! As a therapist, I use the Biblical principles presented here to help other Christians make and sustain spiritual breakthroughs. These same principles will also help you be the person you long to be. You, too, can gain hope and encouragement from the many others who also found hope and made amazing breakthroughs in their lives. As a result of making these changes, they are now living powerful Christian lives. The breakthroughs you make will also be a testimony to God's power. He provides the power, and we do the work.

## Cognitive Behavioral Therapy

I use a psychotherapeutic approach called Cognitive Behavioral Therapy (CBT). This approach began several decades ago and has proven to be very useful in helping people deal with common yet debilitating disorders such as depression, anxiety, personality, and substance abuse disorders. CBT has also proven to be very effective in dealing with a host of other clinical issues that Christians face such as behavior modification, low self-esteem, co-dependency, relationship problems, and phobias. CBT interventions can be used to identify worldly and sinful thoughts and behaviors and replace them with more spiritual ones. CBT is widely practiced in the world of psychology. One reason I like the approach so much is that there is no one "right" way to apply the principles. CBT provides simple interventions that will help you identify the negative thoughts and feelings that drive your behaviors. The interventions you learn will help you gain awareness of why you think the way you think, why you feel the way you feel, and why you do even what you hate to do. The goal of this awareness is to lead you to accept your worldly thoughts and behaviors and take the necessary actions to change. I use CBT with my clients for several reasons. The most important reason is because it fits the Bible. Throughout the Bible, God tells His people why they must think differently and how to do so. This different way of thinking leads to a different emotional response and can lead to different behavior. One goal of CBT is to identify the negative thoughts that create negative emotions which lead to undesired behaviors. In this book, I will help you identify the unspiritual thoughts that create negative emotions which drive sinful behaviors. To make a breakthrough in any behavior, we must view and feel differently about that behavior.

Using Bible-based CBT interventions, you can develop new ways of thinking and feeling about anything. These new thought patterns are developed by identifying the previous worldly view of something and replacing it with a more godly perspective. This more spiritual perspective comes from God's view, as expressed in the Bible. Once the undesirable thoughts are identified, they can be replaced with new ones that are more spiritual. The entire process is much easier to describe than execute, but I have seen this approach work thousands of times. Many Christians attempt to change a behavior without addressing the thoughts and feelings that drive the behavior. This approach did not work for me. The changes are short-lived and do not last long-term. This poor approach may be a major reason why you can make short-term changes but do not sustain them. The goal is to think more spiritually. These more spiritual thoughts will, in turn, produce a better emotional response to any given situation, resulting in more spiritual behavior.

For example, Jesus tells us to not worry, be afraid, or feel anxious. We gravitate to these distressing emotions based upon how we perceive a certain situation. Due to their difficulty to manage, many Christians deal with these emotions using worldly and sinful methods. The consequences of the behavior used to manage these emotions will generally cause more distress. Emotions like guilt and shame may grow increasingly entangled in this cocktail of feelings. Now the cycle starts over, but it is more intense. We view our behaviors as unacceptable, and this causes more emotional distress. The chaotic and ever-increasing malaise, in turn, causes more sinful behaviors. At the end of each cycle, we do not end up in the same place we started. Now we are a bit deeper in a spiritual hole. If repeated, this process creates a downward spiral which can result in, what we call in the world of addictions, "bottom." Some bottoms are lower than others. You know you have hit bottom when you will do whatever it takes to change. As they say in Alcoholics Anonymous, you will go to any lengths to get better.

## Downward Spiral

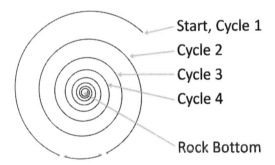

Start, Cycle 1
Cycle 2
Cycle 3
Cycle 4

Rock Bottom

Jesus gives us peace instead of worry, anxiety and fear. We cannot have the peace Jesus promised as long as we think like the world around us. As we learn to think more like Jesus, we will experience the peace of Jesus and begin acting more like Him. Take a look around you. Do you see people at peace? I see quite the contrary. The problem is that many believers are trying to experience the emotional peace of Jesus while thinking like the world. As Christians, we can *learn* how to have this peace even in troubled times. I emphasize the word *learn* because the peace of Jesus does not come naturally, and we must learn from Him how to gain this peace of mind.

Another important principle to understand is that change begins in the mind. Many people who attempt to make spiritual breakthroughs often start with trying to change a behavior. Although this approach seems logical, changing a behavior starts with changing the thinking about the behavior. Thoughts and feelings drive behaviors. The secret to making breakthroughs is to capture the thoughts that create the feelings and drive the behaviors. Sometimes, the negative thought patterns we try to change are irrational yet well ingrained and entrenched. We can respond to irrational thoughts like they are real. For example, if you believe the statement "God is out to get me," you will be filled with anxiety. During the course of therapy, I help believers identify these irrational thoughts and replace them with Biblical truths. Once the individual changes the thought patterns, their emotions change and are much easier to manage. The negative behaviors used to cope with the negative emotions are no longer necessary. The result is that the individual can now change these negative behaviors and evolve into a more spiritual person.

# Chapter 7

# Interventions

### ✍

## More Than a Show

The term "intervention" gained popularity due to a television show bearing this name. Each therapeutic approach involves interventions, a clinical term for a technique to help promote a desired change. I use several common interventions that you have probably already tried. Some are very basic, like reading the Bible, praying, and getting help from others. I also use interventions you probably have not tried. I found that in order to make spiritual breakthroughs, I had to take a different approach. Some of these approaches may seem uncomfortable, but they are not life-threatening. I ask many tough questions. Jesus asked a lot of difficult questions, such as, "Who do people say I am?" And, "Why do you call me 'Lord, Lord,' and do not do what I say?" The answer to these questions will dictate how we respond to Him. How we respond to Jesus will determine how successful we will be in making breakthroughs. This Socratic approach reveals hearts and challenges a way of thinking. These are good questions for you to answer now. If Jesus is Lord, then buckle up, because He will take you places you never dreamed. Following Jesus took me to five continents and many scary places in remote villages and massive cities. Following Jesus led me to see poverty I never thought imaginable and encounter various cultures and unusual people. It also revealed the dark places in my heart and mind I did not want to go. I loved the call to go and make disciples because I could focus on others. I was weary of the call to be a disciple at times because I had to focus on me.

Jesus also asked people to try new ways of doing things. For example, in John 21 the disciples fished all night and did not catch anything. Jesus tells them to try something simple, casting the net on the other side of the boat. The result is a catch so massive that the nets began to break. Sometimes a simple change, like reading different things from the Bible or praying persistently, can have a huge impact.

Another intervention strategy in CBT is to focus on solutions. The Lord asks people to focus on the solution rather than the problem. Many Christians stay stuck because they are problem-focused. A case in point is the feeding of the five thousand, a story told in all four gospels (Matthew 14, Mark 6, Luke 9 and John 6). The disciples asked Jesus to send the crowds away, so the people could go get something to eat. Jesus, however, told the disciples to feed the crowd. Imagine their amazement at His response. Philip is so immersed in the problem; he calculates that eight months wages is not enough to buy bread to feed the crowd. He sees the problem from every angle and does not see a solution from any angle. I often took this approach and find that many Christians do the same. I could analyze a problem to death and recite the problem even if I had just woken up from a coma. I often lived in the problem and suffered from what I call "paralysis of analysis." The disciples asked Jesus to fix the problem, and He put it back on them. You will be in similar situations. Your natural inclination, at times, will be to fixate on the problem and expect God to fix it for you. He may tell you that you have the resources you need. Combining your resources with God's power allows spiritual breakthroughs to occur.

One intervention I use, asking individuals to develop a list of strengths, makes many Christians uncomfortable. They often respond that they have very few if any. I always disagree. The individual may not be able to find them, but they exist because God carefully placed them there. One reason so many Christians feel badly about themselves is because they view themselves in a negative way. This situation occurs because they are focused on their weaknesses and problems and therefore have lost sight of their many strengths. Christians, at times, can even deny that they have strengths. Just because they cannot find these God given assets and are not utilizing them does not negate their existence. These strengths are manifested in accomplishments throughout their life. Many of their strengths are buried under what I call "the rubble of life." This rubble is a result of many of the storms in life such as abuse of some kind from their past, poor decisions, the negative consequences of an addiction, wounds from relationship problems, and mental health issues like anxiety, depression, and a host of other things. An exciting part of the breakthrough process is uncovering these strengths, tapping into them, and utilizing them for God's good purposes.

In therapy, I use what I call the "MacGyver approach." In this old action-adventure television show, the star, MacGyver, was always in some seemingly impossible situation. He may have been trapped in a closet with nothing but bandages and bubble gum but would escape by making a bomb. He used available resources to obtain the desired outcome. In the same way, we need to use our God-given strengths to escape our weaknesses. Right now, these strengths may be channeled in a negative direction, but they are still strengths. For example, most people consider stubbornness to be a weakness. I disagree. Once harnessed and channeled in a positive direction, this same quality is called determination. Stubbornness is just determination turned inside out. Take some time to identify your strengths. If necessary, get help from those who know you well. As we go through the process, we will utilize them to help you make the spiritual breakthroughs you desire. Combining your strengths with God's power creates synergy that causes breakthroughs.

## Are You Focusing on Weaknesses?

Focusing on problems robs us of joy and peace and can keep us awake at night. The problem-focused approach makes us anxious and irritable and causes great distress. Jesus did not ignore the problem as some Christians choose to do. His approach to problem-solving worked, and as Christians, we can imitate His approach. We cannot expect miraculous outcomes with a worldly approach. My prayer is that this book will help you take a more solution-focused approach to life and help you realize all that you have at your disposal to make the breakthroughs you want. Sometimes Jesus will call us to do the seemingly impossible. Our response may be an emotion of feeling overwhelmed, but He will show us how to do it. Jesus will constantly show you that you are capable of doing more than you think you can do.

## Comfort Zone

Another intervention I use is to get people to recreate their comfort zone. God is constantly creating new things, so He can recreate your comfort zone. Our nature is to want change to be easy and comfortable. If the changes you want to make were easy, you would not need this book. You would have made them by now. You may not be happy where you are in your current spiritual state, but you are probably comfortable. Humans love comfort, and we all have a comfort zone. I tried to stay comfortable while emerging from my comfort zone. This approach does not work. I also tried asking God to work on me while in my comfort zone. This approach also failed. You must understand that, by definition, you cannot be comfortable coming out of your comfort zone.

If you are comfortable where you are, God is waiting on you to move forward. He is calling you out of your comfort zone, just as He called Abraham and Sarah out of theirs. They gave up life in the city and a stable home for a new life of wandering and dwelling in tents. God called Moses out of his comfort zone of herding sheep to lead His people. If they would have stayed in their comfort zone, they would not have become heroes of faith. Are you listening to God's call for you to come out of your comfort zone? Will you answer? You cannot answer if you are not listening. For some, God's call started years ago, but you are ignoring it. Thankfully, He keeps calling back. We hear the call, at times, when we go to church or read the Bible. We may keep saying to ourselves something like, "Someday I'm going to answer the call." Make today that day.

Now that I have established the therapeutic approach and explained some of the interventions, it is time for you to write some goals. If we aim at nothing, we will hit it every time. Some goals are very measurable. For example, you may want to lose a specific number of pounds. It will be easy to determine if you achieve the goal or not by stepping on a scale. Other goals are not as measurable. Perhaps you want be to become more spiritual. That's a nice goal, but you will need to explain what that looks like. In other words, how will you know if you accomplish the goal? Describe your desired spiritual breakthroughs in terms as specific as possible. Goals may include changing certain ways of thinking, managing emotions in healthier ways, or stopping a particular behavior. Your goals should be aspirations that will ultimately result in you growing closer to becoming the masterpiece God created you to be.

**Being God's Masterpiece**

In many cases, spiritual breakthroughs go beyond the basic interventions of repenting, praying, reading the Bible, or having more faith. Many Christians become hopeless for making breakthroughs because these interventions are not enough for them. These are often the steps and the direction provided when facing the Goliaths in their life. Many Christians are frustrated and can become hopeless because they have tried this approach multiple times, and it did not result in a breakthrough. This outcome may not seem to make sense on the surface, but stay with me. These interventions are very appropriate and necessary, but sometimes, a different approach is required in order to see breakthroughs. We need an approach to change that builds upon steps such as prayer and Bible study, but we may also need more. Some Christians need more help because they have been through more in their past. Others need an approach that requires a look at the bigger picture of their life. Do not be distressed that you may need more help; rather, be encouraged that more help is available.

To go where you have never been, you will need to do what you have never done. This book will equip you with the knowledge, skills and tools to build upon the repentance, prayer and faith that you have probably already tried multiple times. The approach to pray more or to repent is generally prescribed by well-meaning and caring people. These individuals, perhaps, have not struggled with the difficult issue that you are facing. These well-intentioned friends are sharing what has worked for them and others. But this book is not about solving everyday problems; it's about making spiritual breakthroughs in those difficult areas that have tormented and even tortured you for years. It provides help with the areas in your life where you keep failing and the things that give you the most shame.

God however, did not create us for lives of shame but of victory. God, our Master, views us as amazing Masterpieces of art:

*For we are God's masterpiece. He has created us anew in Christ Jesus, so we can do the good things he planned for us long ago.*
Ephesians 2:10, NLT

My prayer is that you take God's word and whatever faith you can muster in the moment and go forward from here to become that masterpiece. Become that Mona Lisa or statue of David you have always wanted to be. I pray you see the amazing journey of conquest that lies before you. Decide that you will no longer go through the motions of the nothingness of this life, and start pursuing the life you know you can live but have been too afraid to try. The victories ahead will not come without struggle. The Lord, Himself, will help you. God is searching your heart right now and sees how badly you want to change. He sees your fear but will strengthen you to be wholehearted for Him. He knows your thoughts of doubt but will make your mind more open and willing for change. I pray this book will be a blessing to you and others you may share it with, so they, too, can live the victorious life promised to God's children. Now that you have started on the journey, keep moving forward, armed with the mindset of victory, a heart of courage, and a renewed vision for the transformation that God has in store for you.

# PART II

# CORE BELIEFS

## Chapter 8

# Change Your View of Change

### Conforming vs. Transforming

*Do not conform any longer to the pattern of this world, but be transformed by the renewing of your mind.*
Romans 12:2a

*As obedient children, do not conform to the evil desires you had when you lived in ignorance.*
I Peter 1:14

As Christians, we are either being conformed to the world around us, or we are being transformed more into the likeness of Christ. The choice is ours. Which process are you in? Both conforming and transforming take a great deal of time and repetition. In this part of the book, I introduce some of the principles you will need to embrace for your transformation. I will also build upon some of these principles in future chapters. Transforming and conforming begin in the mind and are determined by our core beliefs. A core belief is a deeply ingrained principle we hold to that determines how we respond to situations. These beliefs can form early in childhood and continue to develop as we mature. We may adopt them from the Bible, church, society as a whole, our culture, or our family. Some of our core beliefs are healthy and beneficial. A core belief can be based upon the truth of the Scriptures, for example, "in all things God works for the good" (Romans 8:28). With this core belief, one can deal with very difficult life events in a positive way because the individual believes God will create something positive from a negative situation.

Other core beliefs can be unfounded and untrue but will still determine how we react to the world. Even when core beliefs are untrue, we will respond to them as if they are. Core beliefs determine our reality. For example, someone who has a worldly core belief, such as "everyone must love me," will have a great deal of difficulty obtaining the spiritual qualities of joy and peace. Every day is another episode of "Mission Impossible." This person will fail to accomplish the mission of being loved by others on a regular basis. Some will go to extreme lengths attempting to accomplish this mission. The end result is a very tired, frustrated and unhappy person riddled with angst. This core belief conflicts with the Bible. God states that we must love others, not that we must make them love us. Due to multiple failures at this impossible task, the individual can develop another core belief such as, "I am a failure." This untrue and negative core belief can also become part of their psychological structure. The bottom line is that negative and untrue core beliefs will eventually cause great emotional, spiritual and psychological damage.

A very important part of the spiritual breakthrough process will involve changing some of your core beliefs. God helps us create these new core beliefs. He does so by providing Christians with His thoughts through His Word to transform our mind. In order to do better spiritually, we must stop conforming to the world's way of thinking and let

God transform our mind, thoughts and attitudes. There are a few core beliefs you must have in order to see the spiritual breakthroughs you desire. These core beliefs are explained in the next several chapters. There are literally hundreds of examples of negative core beliefs, and all of us have some. Core beliefs can change and must change if we are going to make spiritual breakthroughs. We must trade in our worldly belief system and adopt God's core beliefs. Changing core beliefs can also lead to other breakthroughs, like managing emotions and stopping or starting certain behaviors.

**A More Positive Perspective on Change**

A core belief of many Christians is: "change is scary." People generally feel this way because we are often afraid of what we do not understand. We can also feel afraid when we sense that we are losing control of a situation. I take some time here to explain the process of change in order to alleviate the fear factor. The thought of changing a difficult area of their life fills many Christians with fear and anxiety. As these emotions build, they can quickly become overwhelmed. Some may even experience a panic attack as they think about the changes they need to make. You may be feeling some symptoms of anxiety right now. Increased pulse rate, dry mouth, sweaty palms and difficulty focusing are symptoms of anxiety. These are physiological manifestations of what is going on in your mind. Take courage; God can calm your anxious heart. In spite of your fear and anxiety, keep moving ahead.

One thing that will help make breakthroughs of any kind easier is viewing the process of change differently. This altered view will decrease the fear and anxiety you associate with change. In other words, change the way you view change. Are you confused? Try this little exercise. Substitute the word "change" for another word that means the same thing and see if you feel differently. For example, try substituting the word "growth" for change. Substituting a word with more positive connotations provides you with a different mental perspective of the process. You will, therefore, get a different emotional response. Remember when you were young, and you grew out of your shoes or clothes? Were you upset? No, kids are excited when they are growing physically. We can be happy about the process of change if we view it as growth. What if you viewed the process of change as "maturing?" Who wants to be immature? Can you remember longing for the privileges of maturity, like getting a driver's license? Viewing change as maturing alters your perspective of the process and therefore provokes a different emotional response.

My personal favorite word for change is "transformation." I think one reason Paul was so radically changed was because he embraced the process of change with a very positive attitude. Paul states that we "are being transformed into [Jesus'] likeness with ever-increasing glory" (2 Corinthians 3:18). The Greek word for transformation is metamorphosis, a biological process you probably learned about in your high school science class. Metamorphosis is the process by which a caterpillar turns into a butterfly. The caterpillar is transfigured into a completely different state. There is nothing inherent in a caterpillar that leads us to believe it could transform into a colorful butterfly. I do not understand everything that happens to the little ugly caterpillar in order for this transformation to occur. But I do know that radical changes happen, and the end result is beautiful and wonderful. God wants our transformation into the likeness of Jesus to be exciting, not overwhelming. Try on God's view of change, and you will begin to see miracles occur.

If the word "change" makes you fearful or anxious, you will proceed slowly. Have you ever lost electrical power at night in an unfamiliar place? Sudden darkness in an unfamiliar place can be frightening, and anxiety levels can rise rapidly. In these situations, you probably do not run around. Since the place is unfamiliar, you will most likely walk slowly and deliberately to move about. This same scenario will occur if you view change as unfamiliar. Your emotional response will be fear and anxiety, and you will proceed very cautiously. Slow and deliberate steps toward progress are better than no steps. You will take bigger and faster steps, however, if you can retrain your brain to view change differently. This more positive you are about the process, the more quickly you will proceed.

Consider the following fact about change to help you to see that it is not as unfamiliar as you many think. By this point in your life, you have already changed many things. Even if you have lived in the same place all your life, you went through many changes. You changed schools, friends, interests, relationships and much more. Take the fear and anxiety out of the changes that you desire to make by reflecting upon all the changes you have made thus far. The process of change is more familiar and less fearful than you think. The better you feel about change, the more spiritual breakthroughs you will make. The better you feel about the process of change, the better your results will be. You must be able to push through the fear of change in order to make spiritual breakthroughs. Fear of the unknown can paralyze us, and it holds many Christians back. However, fear can work for you by making you rely more upon God. David wrote about addressing his fear in Psalm 23:

*The LORD is my shepherd, I shall not be in want.*
*He makes me lie down in green pastures,*
*he leads me beside quiet waters,*
*he restores my soul.*
*He guides me in paths of righteousness*
*for his name's sake. Even though I walk*

*through the valley of the shadow of death,*
*I will fear no evil,*
*for you are with me;*
*your rod and your staff,*
*they comfort me.*
Psalm 23: 1-4

David believed that God was leading him, and David allowed Him to do so. Sometimes God led David to the places he wanted to go, like lush fields and peaceful pools. At other times, God led him to the valley of death. Either way, David knew it was God leading him. Right now, God is leading you to change. However, you must go through the valley to stand upon the mountain of God where spiritual breakthroughs occur. Staying in the valley leads to spiritual decay. Sadly, many Christians take up residence in the valley of mediocrity and the status quo. Their fear of change paralyzes them, and they are stuck spiritually. David gave his fear to God and was therefore comforted. David allowed his fear to make him more God-reliant. You can do the same. When you give God your fear, He gives you comfort. I will make that trade any day. Faith overcomes fear. Give God your fear about the changes you want to make. He will, in turn, lead you to the victories and the breakthroughs you desire.

Fear is a powerful emotion that brings the entire breakthrough process to a halt. I introduce the concept of overcoming fear here and will revisit it later. Fear is one of those constant distractions that must be continuously addressed. Face your fears about change in general for now. Dealing with your fears now will help you to deal with future fears that lay ahead. This is a great opportunity to change the old core belief of "change is scary." Your new core belief can now be: "change is exciting, thrilling, and exhilarating." In order to make the spiritual breakthroughs you desire, you must change your view of change.

## Chapter 9

# Change Your Expectations

❧

*The thief comes only to steal and kill and destroy; I have come that they may have life, and have it to the full.*
John 10:10

W hen pondering life to the full, you may think, "that would be nice." What Christian would not want a full life? Despite these clear words of Jesus in John 10:10, how many Christians can honestly say they expect to have a full life? You may be thinking, "I have a full life — full of problems, struggles and trouble." A common core belief amongst Christians is that the full life Jesus promises is for others and not them.

What is a full life, anyway? I do not believe a life full of problems is what Jesus had in mind for His people when He made this promise. The Apostle Paul prayed for the church at Ephesus to "be filled to the measure of all the fullness of God" (Ephesians 3:19). Later in this epistle, Paul states that one of the purposes of the church is to help each part of the body "become mature, attaining to the whole measure of the fullness of Christ" (Ephesians 4:13). Fullness, however, does not just happen when we become a Christian.

It comes with maturity, which is a process, not an event. Both fullness and maturity require making and sustaining lots of spiritual breakthroughs. So let us get back to the question above. Is the full life fact or fiction for you? Is the full life your expectation? Is the phrase, "I can have a full life in Christ," one of your core beliefs? One reason many Christians may lack this core belief is that obtaining the full life is difficult. I cannot argue with that. If the full life were easy, everyone would have it. Difficulty, however, does not mean that this life is impossible, but it will certainly take work on our part.

I previously thought God did not deliver on His promise of a full life, but a few years ago, I came to a different yet life-changing conclusion. I realized that I was focused on my problems rather than God's promises, and I was allowing Satan to steal the full life promised to me. One way I allowed Satan to steal this full life was by not believing a full life to be possible. My core belief was: "the full life is a myth." I blamed God for my lack of fullness. Once I accepted responsibility for allowing Satan to steal this life from me, I embraced pursuing this full life. Blaming God for your lack of fullness will also keep you stagnant. I decided to stop being a victim of the thief and fight back. When we oppose Satan by believing in God's Word, we will see the promises of God come true.

**Full and Then Some**

Making and sustaining spiritual breakthroughs leads us to this full life. I want to keep making more spiritual breakthroughs in order to increase this fullness. How about you? Jesus did not sacrifice His life for us to have a somewhat full life or partially full life, but completely full. Who among you settles for half of a paycheck when you were promised all of it? Who settles for a small fry when you super-sized?

Even our lives can be super-sized, so full that they overflow with various spiritual qualities. Examine the verses below:

Hope:
*May the God of hope fill you with all joy and peace as you trust in him, so that you may overflow with hope by the power of the Holy Spirit.*
Romans 15:13

Comfort:
*For just as the sufferings of Christ flow over into our lives, so also through Christ our comfort overflows.*
2 Corinthians 1:5

Thankfulness:
*So then, just as you received Christ Jesus as Lord, continue to live in him, rooted and built up in him, strengthened in the faith as you were taught, and overflowing with thankfulness.*
Colossians 2:6-7

Love:
*May the Lord make your love increase and overflow for each other and for everyone else, just as ours does for you.*
I Thessalonians 3:12

Overflowing means completely full and then some. An overflowing life sounds nice, but do you feel like this life is impossible? It is — if we try to accomplish it our way. An overflowing life is only possible with the God of the impossible. Did you just feel your doubt kick back in? Do you feel overwhelmed, knowing all of the changes it will take for you to experience this overflowing life? Are you tempted right now to set this book aside and read something more light-hearted? More entertaining? Less challenging? All of these thoughts and feelings are very normal, but they are the same thoughts and feelings that stopped you before. You must learn to work through these negative thoughts and feelings in order to make spiritual breakthroughs. Nothing changes if nothing changes. What I mean is; if we keep on doing what we have been doing, we will keep getting the same results we have been getting. If you quit forging ahead when you feel anxious, afraid or overwhelmed, you will stay the same.

You can change your negative core belief about this promise of God as I did. The full life for me seemed equivocal to the existence of extraterrestrials, Bigfoot or the Loch Ness Monster. These creatures are supposedly sighted but never captured. I had glimpses of this full life but could not manage to grasp it. What is your expectation from life? Obtaining the full life is purposeful, not accidental. Jesus came to give it to us, but we must become and think more like Him to get it. We experience fullness as we let go of the empty life the world has to offer. As we let go of the unspiritual, we now have space for the spiritual to enter.

I want to see God's promise of the overflowing life become a reality. In spite of the length or difficulty of the journey, I strive each day towards that vision. Do you? The lessons in this book will help you take major steps in a positive direction to see God's vision for your life come true. For you to see God's vision of this full life fulfilled, you may need to make many spiritual breakthroughs. Don't settle for where you are now spiritually, and don't settle for less than what God promised. Raise your expectations to what you can become. God promises that our lives can be full, and all of His promises are true. To receive it, we must believe it. An exciting adventure of growth and change awaits you as you continue your quest for this full, and even overflowing, life.

## Chapter 10

# Let Go of the Status Quo

When we change our expectations about life, we can let go of the status quo. Status quo is not a Biblical term. However, many Christians hold to an unspiritual core belief that says: "the status quo is how I go." They may not verbalize it, but the motto is portrayed in their lifestyle. They blend in rather than standing out or stepping up. They are like spiritual chameleons who change colors to fit into their surroundings. They alter their behaviors to fit their environment rather than changing their heart and mind to confront their environment. When asked about changing something difficult in their life, they may respond with, "that's the way I've always been." Somewhere in life, they adopted the core belief that staying the same is the expectation. We must understand that status quo is not God's expectation. His people are not created or designed to remain the same. We are designed and programmed for growth and change. God designed and equipped us to make and sustain spiritual breakthroughs.

As God's children and His workmanship, we are designed to be masterpieces, not mantle pieces. Masterpieces are amazing works of art, but they take time to create. On a trip to Florence, Italy, a few years ago, my wife and I saw Michelangelo's famous statue of David. The photos of this incredible piece of art do not do it justice. This marble sculpture is more than 17 feet high and weighs over six tons. The sculpture is so lifelike that I stared at it for several minutes waiting for it to breathe. When creating this celebrated piece of art, Michelangelo chiseled away at a massive block of marble day by day for over three years. As a master sculptor, he had a vision that this unshapely rock could be molded into something splendid. His creative vision was far more beautiful than the rock's original form. Michelangelo transformed the stone into the magnificent and eponymous David. The Master we follow as Christians sculpts minds and hearts of stone into the likeness of His Son. We cannot become what God wants us to be if we hold on to the status quo.

When God created man, He stepped back to look and thought, "it was very good" (Genesis 1:31). That very good work, however, rebelled against God and was corrupted by sin. Thankfully, God is also in the business of re-creation.

*You were taught, with regard to your former way of life, to put off your old self, which is being corrupted by its deceitful desires; to be made new in the attitude of your minds; and to put on the new self, created to be like God in true righteousness and holiness.*
Ephesians 4:22-24

God wants His children to have a new attitude, complete with new core beliefs. He wants us to have a new mental and spiritual approach to life. When we become a Christian, we are recreated spiritually. God does not want this new creation to be ordinary but extraordinary. We must let go of the status quo to become the extraordinary person God wants us to be. Going from ordinary to extraordinary requires change. The Bible is full of examples of people coming to grips with the concept that God expects change. The days of the prophet Ezekiel provide one such example. God's people went into exile because they "conformed to the standards of the nations around [them]" (Ezekiel 11:12). Later, God promised deliverance from captivity and gave His people this promise: "I will give them an undivided heart and put a new spirit in them; I will remove from them their heart of stone and give them a heart of flesh" (Ezekiel 11:19). This new spirit included gaining new core beliefs.

God also promises His children today a new heart and a new mind. As Christians, we are reborn but not fully formed. God, like Michelangelo, takes the chisel and goes to work to create this new heart and mind. This chiseling process is difficult for us because it hurts. The things that make us ordinary, like worldliness, sin, character defects, bad attitudes, negative personality traits and more, must be hammered on daily. God wants *everything* that is not like His Son to be chiseled away. We are ready and willing to let God chisel out some things. All of us have certain aspects of our lives that we are ready to bid good riddance. These parts of our lives cause us great distress, and we may even hate these things about ourselves. However, you may have what I call "pet sins." That's what I called the sins in my life that I did not want to be chiseled out. These are the sins we know are not like Jesus, but we enjoy and, perhaps secretly, long to do them. We see these deceitful desires as pleasurable. God sees them as poison. *All* ungodliness must go, because whatever ungodly thing you hold onto will eventually take over. It took me some time to get serious about dealing with these pet sins. I concluded that if I were to have cancer surgery, I would not want the doctor to leave some cancer behind. Why then would I want to leave anything behind that could kill me spiritually? We make that choice when we cling to the core belief to maintain the status quo. We cannot be a masterpiece if we do not let the Master do the sculpting His way. We are not yet fully formed in Christ, and God needs your cooperation in order to continue His work.

God does not force us to cooperate, but He urges us to. In order to be transformed more into the likeness of Christ, Paul made incredible changes in his heart and mind. The following verse penned by Paul helped me a great deal. I decided to embrace his attitude about allowing God to work on my own heart and mind.

*Therefore, I urge you, brothers and sisters, in view of God's mercy, to offer your bodies as a living sacrifice, holy and pleasing to God—this is your true and proper worship.*
Romans 12:1, NIV

The word Paul uses, translated here as "urge," really means to beg. I realized that God was begging me to allow Him to transform my mind and heart. In order for that to happen, I had to become this living sacrifice. Living sacrifices that keep squirming on the altar are not submitting to God. I realized I was not allowing God to work on me daily the way He wanted to. Jesus was a living sacrifice and allowed God to work in His life daily. Jesus submitted to God at all times; I submitted sometimes. I decided that the status quo must go in *every* part of my life. Are there areas of your life where you have settled for the status quo? If so, God is begging you now to let it go. In what area of Jesus' life did He settle for the status quo? Fear of letting go of the status quo keeps us moving on the altar and dodging the chisel. In order to be the spiritual sacrifice God wants us to be, we must allow Him to work. Spirituality is an inside job. We must learn to think more like Him. When we think like God, we will develop His mind and His heart. In order to renew our minds, we must adopt His core beliefs. When we adopt new core beliefs, we no longer have the need to cling to the status quo.

## God's Thoughts and Ways

Examine this verse, and I will explain how this new thinking occurs:

*"For my thoughts are not your thoughts,*
*neither are your ways my ways,"*
*declares the LORD.*
*"As the heavens are higher than the earth,*
*so are my ways higher than your ways*
*and my thoughts than your thoughts.*
*As the rain and the snow*
*come down from heaven,*
*and do not return to it*
*without watering the earth*
*and making it bud and flourish,*
*so that it yields seed for the sower and bread for the eater,*
*so is my word that goes out from my mouth:*
*It will not return to me empty,*
*but will accomplish what I desire*
*and achieve the purpose for which I sent it."*
Isaiah 55:8-11

In order to become the masterpiece that God wants us to be, we must embrace His vision for us, but too many Christians have erased God's vision for them. We must also embrace His thoughts. To God, the status quo is not a place to stay but a place to flee. To God, pain is profitable, not prohibiting. God knows flaws and failure are not fatal. God can teach us how to think differently about the whole process of change, sacrifice and chiseling, if we allow Him. We cannot make spiritual breakthroughs without first adopting the right attitude about change. I'm sure you've heard the phrase, "attitude is everything." We need to embrace God's thoughts and allow Him to create His masterpiece. We must become a willing sacrifice that submits to His method of making us more spiritual, adopting God's core beliefs and His vision for us. We must have a spiritual mindset to be sculpted into a more spiritual being. The basis of making spiritual breakthroughs is trusting God's vision for us and His core beliefs.

In order to obtain the life that God wants for us, we must understand that He thinks very differently than we do. He has a different attitude about the quality of life we can have as Christians. God has ways to accomplish this life for us that we will not understand. Do not allow the promise from God, presented above from the book of Isaiah, to fall upon deaf ears. His Word is intended to impact us, so we can live the life that He desires for His children. God's word can accomplish what He desires if you let Him. Too many of His children have settled for far less than God planned for them. God has the miraculous in mind, but we often settle for mediocrity.

The Bible states that God is awesome. I had no trouble accepting this fact. For years, however, I rationalized that an awesome God was satisfied with my awful approach to the new life He offered. Since God is awesome, He has a vision for His children, created in his image, to be awesome. The word, "awesome," is so overused today that it is does not describe God adequately. In modern day vernacular, music, movies, meals, and many more mundane things are described as awesome. Maybe we should refer to God as "Most Awesome." The Bible describes the Almighty as God of gods, Lord of lords, mighty and awesome (Deuteronomy 10:17). He performs great and awesome wonders (Deuteronomy 10:21). His majesty is awesome (Job 37:22). He is awesome in glory (Exodus 15:11). His deeds are awesome (Psalm 66:3). His works are awesome on man's behalf (Psalm 66:5). Even His name is awesome (Psalm 99:3).

I may not be doing an awesome job describing the awesomeness of God, but I think you get the point. Since we serve an awesome God, we must develop the core belief that we can do awesome spiritually. You must believe that no matter how poorly you are doing now spiritually, you can be awesome. The Bible is full of examples of this principle. Jesus Christ is the same yesterday, today and forever (Hebrews 13:8). What Jesus did to help people become awesome then is available to us now, yet spiritually, we can settle for awful. If we let Him, God will empower us to boldly live the life He wants for us, instead of a wearisome and sinful life spent pandering to the status quo. A contemporary Christian song entitled "Brave" by Nichole Nordeman addresses this issue as the singer bids "so long" to the status quo. For a link to watch a music video of this song, visit my web site at www.mtccounseling.com. Let the words of this song inspire you, as they do me, to let go of fear and the status quo. God is waiting on you to change your life by changing your mind, your core beliefs, and your heart. As you go through this section about core beliefs, take time to identify some of your unspiritual core beliefs. After completing this task, ask yourself: "Am I ready for God's thoughts to become my thoughts and God's ways to be my ways? Am I willing to let God create in me a new attitude and heart?" If you are willing to let God transform your mind and heart, you are well on your way to the life God promised you.

A core belief we must adopt is that God created us to be awesome and to do awesome spiritually. Ecclesiastes 3:1 states that there is a time for everything under heaven. If you are currently settling for the status quo, time is up; embrace a new era of bravery where fear is not allowed to hold you back. Let our Most Awesome God, through His Word and the words of this song, spur you on to do awesome spiritually. God is not interested in the status quo and wants you to let it go. Will you become the master-piece God intendeds for you to be or settle for being the same? Masterpiece or mantelpiece, the choice is ours. I pray that you embrace God's thoughts and leave your stinking thinking behind. You will not do awesome by accident; it is an attitude that must be made new in your mind.

## Chapter 11

# Change Your View of Impossible

⁓

How many times have you considered changing something, like letting go of the status quo? How many times have you thought about wholeheartedly seeking the full life Jesus promised? How often is your next thought, "that's impossible?" The "impossible" can be broken down into smaller possibilities. Jesus had the core belief that, "what is impossible with men is possible with God" (Luke 18:27). The Bible contains a plethora of examples when something that seems impossible actually happens. The blind receive back their sight, the lame walk, the mute speak, a virgin gives birth, the dead are raised back to life, massive bodies of water are parted, thousands are fed with a young man's lunch, and the list goes on and on. Today, the impossible continues to occur. Christians are successfully confronting addictions, mental health issues, low self-esteem, personality traits, abuse, divorce, disasters, loss of loved ones, unemployment, foreclosure, bankruptcy, family of origin problems, financial difficulties, worry, stress, anxiety, panic attacks, and the list goes on. Did you find something on this list that you thought seemed impossible to surmount? Many Christians, unfortunately, do not believe it's possible to overcome their issues. The God of the impossible disagrees.

Based upon his knowledge of the miracles and teachings of Jesus, Paul developed the following core belief: "I can do everything through him who gives me strength" (Philippians 4:13). Another one of my personal favorites of Paul's core beliefs is, "in all these things we are more than conquerors through him who loved us" (Romans 8:37). Paul's radical transformation was not something that happened to him inadvertently. His transformation was deliberate and began with a different way of thinking. He began to think like Jesus and eventually developed the core belief that nothing was impossible. If a stereotypical, self-righteous Pharisee can become a powerful preacher, then *nothing* is impossible.

A major decision I had to make in order to make and sustain spiritual breakthroughs was to believe God's promises over my feelings. You will need to make the same decision; I continue to make this decision daily. This concept may seem impossible. It is hard to *feel* that these promises are true if you do not *believe* they are true. Once you make the decision to believe *God's* promises over *your* feelings, you will be well on your way to a transformation you never imagined. How long have you used the excuse not to change something because you viewed it as impossible? God is taking that excuse away from you. Thinking something is impossible gives the unspiritual and faint of heart an excuse not to try. Those who want to change find a way, and those who don't find an excuse. Whether you think you can change the impossible or that you cannot, you are correct. Many Christians wish to be different, yet my experience is that wishers do not do the necessary work it requires to be different. When Jesus provided the disciples the opportunity for a miraculous catch, He told them to cast their net on the other side of the boat. Jesus could have caused the fish to jump in the boat. We still have a responsibility to put forth the effort in order for the impossible to occur. God will empower you to do the work necessary for you to make impossible breakthroughs if you allow Him.

Part of the process of making and sustaining spiritual breakthroughs is challenging your previous thinking. Jesus challenged people's thinking throughout his ministry, and he is challenging yours right now. It is time to start thinking outside the worldly box of what is possible and adopt a more spiritual core belief. In order to make and sustain spiritual breakthroughs, we must learn to tap into the divine power available to every Christian. Paul wrote, we "have divine power to demolish strongholds" (2 Corinthians 10:4). Think about that word, demolish. It offers the mental image of a barrier decimated into thousands of tiny pieces. How powerful is divine power? Well, if I told you at this point, your head would likely explode, so we'll discuss more about God's power later in the book. The most entrenched stronghold I needed to demolish in my own life was my unspiritual thinking. My mind was a fortified fortress of unbelief regarding God's capabilities, but His divine power demolished my old way of thinking and redefined impossible. The Bible is full of examples of people who made "impossible" breakthroughs. How did an old man and an old woman whose bodies were as good as dead become parents? How did a man who fled for his life from Egypt later lead the exodus of thousands of slaves in order to give them a new life? How did a frightened man hiding in a winepress turn into a fearless warrior? How did a self-absorbed womanizer become selfless and sacrifice his life to save his country? The principles these men and women used to make spiritual breakthroughs will work for us, too.

If you are reading this book as another attempt to make change easy, you will be disappointed. If this thinking describes your situation, your impossible task is to change your view of difficulty. Change became easier and less frightening when I viewed it from a more spiritual perspective. Making and sustaining spiritual breakthroughs is not easy. Therefore, you may need to get a more spiritual view of all things challenging. In this book, I do not present any "never heard before" or "previously hidden" secrets that make change easier. However, I do present ways to view the impossible differently. Making and sustaining spiritual breakthroughs is hard work but not impossible. Even if it was impossible, *nothing* is impossible with God. "Difficult" does not necessarily need to mean overwhelming, horrible or whatever other extreme negative adjective you use to describe something that isn't easy. Difficulty is what you make of it and can have many advantages. Don't let your fear of hard work talk you out of changing yet again. Face it head on with a new attitude and determination. If making spiritual breakthroughs were easy, more people would be making them. There would be much less sin in the world, and more people would be like Jesus.

Prior to attempting to make a spiritual breakthrough, I hear many Christians exclaim, "I *can't* change!" Sometimes this core belief is yelled or whispered. The volume of the delivery does not really matter. What does matter is that this person spoke the truth. Like Jesus said, "out of the overflow of the heart the mouth speaks" (Matthew 12:34). Sometimes Christians develop the core belief that change is impossible from years of trying and failing. Others lack confidence in God or themselves to bring positive life changes to fruition. Whatever the reason, the statement is not true. According to the Almighty God, nothing is impossible. When I hear a Christian say they can't change, I often respond, "I agree with you." At this point in the conversation, they may feel a sense of relief, assuming I understand their plight and implied powerlessness. A smile may emerge, and tears may cease. Then I clarify, "I believe that you can't change your way." At this point, the smile vanishes, a look comes across their face like I just grew horns, and the tears generally flow again. The river of tears flows heavier this time because, now, they are busted. They know that I know; their way involves comfort, and God's way involves work. They know they are not ready to go where God wants to take them. The conversation can get somewhat heated and emotional at this point. You may be feeling this way yourself, right now. The fact is, the individual *won't* change due to the pain or fear. They won't change because they do not believe they can. Many Christians desire change but are not ready for it. This may be your current situation. Whatever your situation, changing your core beliefs to God's core belief — that all things are possible — is paramount.

## Chapter 12

# Change Your Worldview

*I have told you these things, so that in me you may have peace. In this world you will have trouble. But take heart! I have overcome the world.*
John 16:33

Some Christians think it's impossible for them to overcome the world as Jesus did. This belief stems from an unspiritual worldview. In psychology, "worldview" refers to an individual's overall perspective of the world. It is both conscious and unconscious and determines how the individual interprets and interacts with the world. Some scholars refer to worldview as a "mental map." This map is all-encompassing and determines the individual's approach to dealing with the world around them. Sadly, many Christians do not share the worldview of Jesus that the world can be overcome. Therefore, they feel defeated on a constant basis. I was one of them. As Christians, we live in the world, but the world does not need to control us. Jesus was the light of the world and called His followers to be the same. We cannot be a light to the world if we do not shine. We shine by showing the world how to live righteous lives in unrighteous conditions. We are called out of the kingdoms of this world to be in His Kingdom. It took me some time to understand what Jesus meant by His statement that He overcame the world. I now understand that, as Christians, we can be a part of this world without being overcome or overwhelmed by it.

Jesus also says that in this world we will have trouble. I've never met anyone who disagrees with this statement. However, many Christians are shocked and unprepared for the troubles of this world. As Christians, we live in and respond to this troubled world on a daily basis. Instead of facing these trials, many Christians have the core belief that "I must succumb to the world." I previously believed the peace Jesus promised came through surrendering to the world. Jesus said that peace comes not through surrender but victory. Instead of being overwhelmed, I decided to overcome. My previous core belief told me that peace was the absence of trouble, yet Jesus promised that peace was obtainable in spite of trouble. This peace does not come from calling a truce or a cease-fire with the world. This peace comes from trouncing the world as Jesus did. I previously believed that going to heaven was the only way to overcome the world. Jesus, on the other hand, states that Christians can beat Satan on his home field. For many, the concept of overcoming the world is not even on the radar. These Christians believe that if it is possible, only spiritual superheroes, like the apostles, can do it.

What did Jesus mean by "overcoming the world?" This concept is often very new to some Christians. The Apostle John had much to say about this in his writings and used the word "overcome" fourteen times in his five books in the Bible. I find it interesting that one who overcame so much wrote freely about overcoming. Here are some examples:

*I write to you, young men, because you have overcome the evil one.*
I John 2:13b

*I write to you, young men, because you are strong, and the word of God lives in you, and you have overcome the evil one.*
I John 2:14b

*You, dear children, are from God and have overcome them, because the one who is in you is greater than the one who is in the world.*
I John 4:4

*This is love for God: to obey his commands. And his commands are not burdensome, for everyone born of God overcomes the world. This is the victory that has overcome the world, even our faith. Who is it that overcomes the world? Only he who believes that Jesus is the Son of God.*
I John 5:3-5

The Apostle John did not always have the core belief that he could overcome the world. His actions during the last few days of the life of Jesus demonstrate this point. John, like Peter, fell asleep on Jesus three times in the Garden. He later ran away when the mob came to arrest Him. John, like Peter, was not at the resurrection. When the women returned to the apostles to tell about their encounter with the angel at the empty tomb, John thought it was nonsense. When he and Peter ran to the empty tomb, Peter rushed into it, but John stayed outside. As you can see, John did not always have faith that God could overcome the impossible. The resurrection of Jesus, however, radically changed John's worldview. The "Son of Thunder" wanted to be great but misunderstood that true greatness was victory over the world. On several occasions, John's self-aggrandizing ambition to be "the greatest" was revealed. In Matthew 22, he was prideful and thought he could drink the cup of leadership in Jesus' new Kingdom. He was later humbled and learned otherwise. Prior to this humbling experience, He often argued with the other apostles over who would be the greatest. He later submitted to Peter's leadership after the Lord ascended back to heaven. In Luke 9, the Son of Thunder wanted to call down fire from heaven on the Samaritans who were not receptive to the gospel. After the resurrection, Luke records in Acts 8 that John helped Peter evangelize this area. A different worldview led to a different man. A man full of anger and selfish ambition ultimately became known as "the Apostle of Love." This transformation could not have occurred if he did not believe that he could overcome the world.

How did John come to the core belief that disciples could overcome the world? Here, I believe, is John's train of thought. Jesus was from God and belonged to God. Jesus' power came from God, enabling Jesus to be victorious over the world and rise from the dead. We, as followers of Jesus, come from God and belong to God, so we have the same power available to us. With this greater power, we can overcome the world. This logic may not make sense to you right now, but it is essential to the breakthrough process. You may need to be patient with yourself and let this thinking set in. If you doubt this promise, you will certainly not be the first disciple of Jesus to do so. The eleven other disciples at the Last Supper with John also doubted Jesus at times. Those who worked through their doubt went on to not just to overcome the world but to revolutionize it. God says you can do the same. For John, Jesus was real. Throughout his writings, he used phrases like the following to express his belief, "we have seen His glory" (John 1:14), and "That which was from the beginning, which we have heard, which we have seen with our eyes, which we have looked at and our hands have touched" (I John 1:1). The more real Jesus is for you, the easier it is to adopt His core belief that as Christians we can overcome the world.

**Overcoming Defined**

What does it mean to overcome? Some versions of the Bible translate the word "overcome" to mean to conquer or to be victorious. Simply put, according to one online dictionary, it means to "win, overpower, overwhelm, defeat or to prevail over." John believed he could overcome the world, so he fought to do so. Jesus also believes that you can overcome the world. The more important question in this moment is; do you believe you can? If the answer is no, it is understandable, but take heart from the desperate man in Mark 9 whose son was possessed by an evil spirit.

*So they brought him. When the spirit saw Jesus, it immediately threw the boy into a convulsion. He fell to the ground and rolled around, foaming at the mouth. Jesus asked the boy's father, "How long has he been like this?" "From childhood," he answered. "It has often thrown him into fire or water to kill him. But if you can do anything, take pity on us and help us. 'If you can?'" said Jesus. "Everything is possible for him who believes." Immediately the boy's father exclaimed, "I do believe; help me overcome my unbelief!"*
Mark 9:20-24

Right now, you may be exclaiming the same thing: "Help me overcome my unbelief!" This man overcame his unbelief by accepting Jesus at His word, and his son was healed. You can overcome your unbelief in the same way. Accepting Jesus at His word will also help you overcome the world. Let me make this concept more practical. Simply put, it means not to be controlled by thoughts, emotions and behaviors that can control you and often "throw you into fire and water." You need to overcome your unbelief that you do not need to be controlled by sin, your past, your circumstances, your disorder, your attitudes, your emotions, or whatever else may be controlling you at the present time.

A myriad of troubles can control Christians and rob us of the peace that Jesus promised. For example, you may now be controlled by a particular sin such as selfishness, pride, lust, and arrogance (my "big four"). You pray and repent, yet these sins continue to control you. To make things worse, these sins do not attack in isolation. They can gang up on you like a pack of wolves and attack you on a daily basis. They also leave a wake of devastation in their path. Suffering continuous defeats to these sins can lead to spiritual, psychological and emotional damage and despair.

We can also allow external situations, such as medical conditions, to control our attitudes, emotions and behaviors. These conditions can hinder or impair our physical ability, but they do not need to control our attitude. Mental health conditions like mood and anxiety disorders affect millions of Christians each year. Some people allow these disorders to define them. What I mean is that they *are* a depressed person rather than a person with depression. In other words, they allow depression to dictate their behaviors rather than Christ. The depression becomes the standard for their actions rather than the Bible. Others may have a physical disability or handicap and refer to themselves as "disabled" or "handicapped," rather than a person with a disability or a handicap. Defining ourselves outside of the realm of a spiritual context will not enable us to overcome the world. This worldly definition will also rob us of the peace Jesus promised.

Perhaps there is a personality trait which dominates your life such as being too controlling, too dependent, or too independent. These traits can severely damage relationships and self-esteem. Maybe you want to be liked too much or get too much gratification from being needed and helping others. Perhaps you have issues with co-dependency. Maybe your past is haunting you and robbing you of peace. All of these situations can be overcome by the power of God. We must tap into that power if we are to claim the promise. Some Christians are controlled by a negative behavior such as drinking, drugging, pornography, promiscuity, gambling, online gaming, and others. These behaviors can eventually take over the individual's life. There is a great deal of guilt and shame connected to these behaviors that can also control our view of our self and our emotional makeup. These issues, too, can be overcome by the power of God.

To you, this discussion may seem to be about semantics, but all too often, the conditions and disorders mentioned define our worldview. Rather than letting God define our view of the world, we can allow the world to define it for us. Christians often allow a limitation or weakness to define them, and they begin to interpret the world through that limitation. Whatever defines you controls you, so do not let worldly characteristics, like a physical, mental, or emotional condition, define you. Be defined by the spiritual. We cannot overcome the world if we allow the world to define us. Too many discouraged and defeated Christians allow themselves to be defined by these conditions. Many once confident and brave warriors are now hiding in caves and clefts just as the Israelites did in the times of the Judges. The Israelites were called to conquer a people who turned around and conquered them because of their unspiritual condition. Many Christians have stopped the fight and begun the flight back to worldly ways of thinking and behaving. You cannot make spiritual breakthroughs without a more spiritual approach. A breakthrough that many Christians need to make is to change their worldview and believe they can overcome it.

**The Call to Overcome**

Jesus overcame sin, death, hell and the grave. As you can tell by the following verses, Jesus is serious about His followers emerging victorious. Are you serious about it?

Helping Christians overcome the world was very important to John and Jesus. We must make and sustain spiritual breakthroughs to claim this promise. Look at what Jesus gives those who overcome (the following bold emphasis is added):

*To him who **overcomes**, I will give the right to eat from the tree of life, which is in the paradise of God.*
Revelation 2:7

*He who **overcomes** will not be hurt at all by the second death.*
Revelation 2:11

*To him who **overcomes**, I will give some of the hidden manna. I will also give him a white stone with a new name written on it, known only to him who receives it.*
Revelation 2:17

*To him who **overcomes** and does my will to the end, I will give authority over the nations—*
Revelation 2:26

*He who **overcomes** will, like them, be dressed in white. I will never blot out his name from the book of life, but will acknowledge his name before my Father and his angels.*
Revelation 3:5

*Him who **overcomes** I will make a pillar in the temple of my God. Never again will he leave it. I will write on him the name of my God and the name of the city of my God, the new Jerusalem, which is coming down out of heaven from my God; and I will also write on him my new name.*
Revelation 3:12

*To him who **overcomes**, I will give the right to sit with me on my throne, just as I **overcame** and sat down with my Father on his throne.*
Revelation 3:21

The head of the church wrote a letter to these specific churches about overcoming the world. Jesus told His apostles in Matthew 16 that His kingdom will prevail against the gates of hell. His expectations did not change by the time John wrote the book of Revelations and have not changed for His current-day disciples. His church cannot accomplish this mission to prevail against the gates of Hades if its members don't believe they can overcome the world. My experience is that most Christians do not share these core beliefs of Jesus about His church. His kingdom can only overcome the world and triumph over the gates of hell if the citizens of His kingdom embrace these core beliefs. Do you have these core beliefs? If not, Jesus is calling you to embrace them. He will also help you overcome your unbelief and the fears that hold you back.

### Repentance

The word, "overcome," appears seven times in the seven letters to the churches in Revelation 2-3. The word repent, meaning a change of mind for the better, occurs six times in these same letters. Repentance is the precursor to overcoming spiritual obstacles. This better state of mind will lead you to improved feelings and behaviors. However, repentance is not a one-time occurrence. For me, this change of mind needs to occur daily, if not multiple times per day. Let times of refreshing begin as you repent and develop a new and healthier attitude about overcoming this world as Jesus did.

You can begin changing some thought patterns now. Do you believe you can be victorious over sin, your past or your circumstances? If not, this explains why you haven't seen victories. We can't be triumphant over these foes if we do not imitate the conquerors before us, like John. What steps do you need to take to gain this core belief? John changed his worldview, and his world changed. He, in turn, was able to change the world. As you change your worldview, your world and the world of others will also change.

## Chapter 13

# Obstacle or Opportunity?

*❧*

J esus said, "In this world you will have trouble" (John
16:33), and your view of these troubles will help determine your response. The process of change offers many
chances to view situations as either obstacles or opportunities. Our corresponding emotional response, positive
or negative, can either expedite or impede our progress.
Knowing that our conditioned emotional response to obstacles and opportunities is very different, we need to learn
to view obstacles in a more favorable light. Changing our
perspective of an obstacle changes our emotional response.
Every obstacle we face is an opportunity for God to work
and gives us a front row seat to watch the power of God
do miracles. A negative emotional response to change and
obstacles can keep us stagnant, ensnared by sin and other
bad habits.

A great example of people who viewed God-given
opportunities as obstacles are the Hebrew slaves Moses led
out of Egypt. Their story illustrates how viewing change
and obstacles negatively can create a negative emotional
response and a negative outcome. These slaves needed to be
made new in the attitude of their minds. They floundered

spiritually as their thoughts diverged from God's plans. The Promised Land was a promise from God to the His people, but it was not handed to them on a silver platter. They had to work for it, enduring troubles and hardships along the way. God's people faced many challenging situations that they viewed as obstacles. Moses' first task was to get a million people out of Egypt. This was certainly no small task, but God delivered His people by sending ten plagues upon the nation of Egypt. The next big challenge was the Red Sea. God parted it, so His people could cross over safely. Difficulties like crossing the Jordan River and conquering the land's current inhabitants followed. God's people needed to make spiritual breakthroughs and overcome their fears in order to seize the land promised to them. Their fear was a direct result of viewing opportunities as obstacles. The Israelite nation is a lasting example of what happens when God's followers succumb to fear. We can only inherit God's will for our lives when we overcome these negative emotions.

Fear sneaks into our peripherals when we view a situation as an obstacle rather than an opportunity for God to deliver us. Fear prevents many Christians from making spiritual breakthroughs and living life to the fullest. Many Christians miss out on their own personal Promised Land by allowing fear and other negative emotions to paralyze them. The generation of Hebrews who were emancipated from Egypt viewed God's opportunities as obstacles and became extremely afraid. God promised the Israelites, "a good and spacious land, a land flowing with milk and honey" (Exodus 3:8). This land was an opportunity to provide His people with a fresh start and a chance to live free and apart from other nations. His people, on the other hand, viewed the same situation quite differently as they grew weary of wandering through the desert and worried about battling the land's current inhabitants. God's thoughts were not their thoughts. Their unspiritual view of the situation severely hindered their ability to take up residence this new land.

In Numbers 13, God commands Moses to send a man from each tribe to explore the Promised Land. After 40 days, they returned with a discouraging report. The cities were fortified and very large, and the people were so powerful and of such great size that the Israelites seemed like grass-hoppers. The Hebrews had the opportunity to be faithful, but they chose to be fearful. We can also make the same mistake, not viewing obstacles as an opportunity for God to work. In their mind, the obstacles were bigger than God could handle. In spite of previous miracles, they shrunk God and minimized His power. The times in my life when I minimized God and maximized my problems did not turn out well. This approach didn't end well for that generation of Hebrews either.

The Israelites needed a double dose of faith and courage to believe that God could use this obstacle as an opportunity to show His great power. Their disbelief did not go unpunished. The consequence? The Israelites roamed the desert for the next forty years. The generation that witnessed the miracles of the exodus did not have the faith to get to the Promised Land. There are consequences in our lives, too, when we fail to view obstacles as opportu-nities. Failure to do so can lead to several difficult emotions such as anger, frustration, discouragement and hopeless-ness. Some Christians wander spiritually for years struggling with these emotions. The cycle of trying to change, failing, feeling discouraged, and coping with these negative emo-tions in an unspiritual manner can go on for years. This cycle can be better explained as a downward spiral. Each time the cycle is completed, the individual is more down spiritually and emotionally than when the cycle began. After each rotation, faith and hope for change is diminished. It is time to trade in the old cycle for a new one, an upward spiral that leads to God and positive changes. Obstacles are God's opportunity for us to grow, not something that should stop us from being the person God wants us to be. We must learn to view every obstacle as an opportunity for God to work. Maturing as a Christian is about breaking the old cycle and knocking down any barriers that hinder growth. These obstacles may be different for each one of us, but the process of overcoming them works the same. In order to make and sustain breakthroughs, you must believe that barriers to spiritual growth can be broken down. You have already overcome some obstacles up to this point in your life, or you would not be reading a book on how to break through more. Building on past victories is essential to breaking the old cycle of downward spirals. Prior victories over a bear and a lion gave David the confidence to face Goliath. The men and women in the Bible who viewed obstacles as opportunities went on to do amazing things for God. Those who did not are valuable examples of what can happen when we do not allow God to transform our minds.

Take some time to evaluate the challenges in your life. Are you viewing them as obstacles or opportunities? When God's thoughts become your thoughts, you will see these challenges as opportunities for Him to work. Make the decision now to change your perspective and adopt this new core belief.

## Chapter 14

# Change Your Attitude about Comfort and Suffering

*Not only so, but we also rejoice in our sufferings, because we know that suffering produces perseverance; perseverance, character; and character, hope. And hope does not disappoint us, because God has poured out his love into our hearts by the Holy Spirit, whom he has given us.*
Romans 5:3-5

### The Cost of Comfort

I remember wrestling with the quote, "rejoice in our sufferings," for the first time. I had read this passage many times before but never really tried to grasp the deeper meaning. Let it suffice to say that in my early years as a Christian, I settled for a cursory understanding of some of God's core beliefs. Initially, this statement made absolutely no sense to me at all. I asked myself, "why in the world would I ever want to think this way about suffering, and even if I could, how is it possible?" When we wrestle with the deep truths of the Word, God will lead us to a better understanding of how His ways benefit us. We will not change our core beliefs about suffering until we change our beliefs about comfort. As long as comfort is king, suffering will be the serf. I will come back to this verse shortly and explain it more thoroughly. Before we learn to rejoice in sufferings, however, let me first address our concept of the comfort zone. God believes that comfort is overrated. God wants His children to be comforted, not necessarily comfortable.

Needless to say, it is a lot more comfortable to stay the same than it is to change. The comfort of the familiar is less threatening than the great unknown of change. Sadly, many Christians embrace the core beliefs of "comfort is king" or "comfort at all cost." They may not tattoo these slogans on their body, but you see evidence in their life. Our culture preaches comfort in every area of our life. Society proffers beverages, hotel chains, furniture and foods all named for comfort. Conforming to this never-ceasing message of comfort keeps many Christians stagnant. Change and comfort rarely coexist. The truth is that change is uncomfortable, and there is no comfortable way to make a breakthrough. You may have already tried many easier and softer ways to change. Perhaps, by now, you are convinced that the comfortable way does not pay. You may be realizing that a major spiritual breakthrough is going to cause some discomfort. Let me be more direct; it is going to cause a lot of discomfort, and frankly, you will find it to be painful. You will not have a good attitude about the process of making a breakthrough until you view suffering as beneficial.

In order to make the breakthroughs I desired, I had to change a couple of my ingrained core beliefs. "Pursue pleasure with passion" was a part of my life's mission statement. This core belief led to all kinds of sinful behaviors with negative consequences. The behaviors and subsequent consequences were destructive to me spiritually, emotionally and physically. A second core belief I had was "practice pain avoidance." Procrastination is the best way I found to implement this life principle. I now understand that procrastination ultimately leads to more pain. My pleasure-seeking and pain-avoidance mindset had to change in order to make the spiritual breakthroughs I wanted to achieve. I came to the conclusion that the cost of comfort was too high. The pursuit of comfort kept me the same. Embracing the benefits of suffering resulted in radical changes. The cost of a life of comfort was ultimately the one thing I was avoiding, more pain.

## The Value of Suffering

I do not enjoy going to the dentist because he always seems to find some new way to inflict pain. One thing I appreciate about my dentist is that he is honest. When he says, "this is going to hurt," he is always right. Gentle dental is an oxymoron. Sometimes the pain is immediate, and sometimes it is delayed; but it always comes. Yet I shudder to think of where my dental health would be if I did not decide to face some pain along the way. How would your mental health be better if you faced some pain along the way? Would you have better self-esteem? Would you be less anxious or depressed? Would you still be addicted to a substance? How would your spiritual health be better? Would you be closer to God and others if you made the changes necessary to obtain these goals? How would your physical health be improved? Would you weigh less and be in better shape? Would you fit into a smaller dress or pants size? I think you now see there are some rewards to suffering.

Suffering is part of the narrow road that leads to the small gate where Jesus wants to take us. It is also a part of the paths of righteousness that David spoke about in the Psalms. Eventually, I arrived at the conclusion that there is no comfortable way to follow a Savior who was familiar with suffering. I decided that Jesus understood the value of suffering, and He was trying to teach it to me. Suffering is the breeding ground for humility and, ultimately, more spirituality. Right now, you may have difficulty grasping the value of suffering. If so, you are not alone. Many Christians have the core belief that "suffering is bad." This belief comes straight from the world and must be addressed if you are to proceed with making spiritual breakthroughs. The One who suffered for us on the cross knew the value of suffering. He wants to teach that to His followers. Are you ready to change your view of suffering?

## Positive and Negative Pain

You've heard the phrase, "no pain, no gain." These words are probably somewhere in every gym in America. Gym rats and muscle heads often overuse the term, but it is appropriate and applicable for this discussion. Women use a similar term when they yell — "Feel the burn!" — in aerobics or spin classes. Every athlete knows that training must hurt to be effective. However, outside of the world of sports, there is little discussion on the benefits of pain. In the sports world, trainers and physical therapists realize that there are different types of pain. Negative pain leads to injury and must be avoided. Positive pain leads to greater strength and improved performance. An athlete's ability to endure this positive pain can make them into a champion. If athletes avoid this type of pain, they will never be transformed from chump to champ.

As Christians, we must realize that there are different types of pain. As with the athlete, positive pain leads to growth. The pain that you experience from addressing your issues and making changes is positive pain. You may be in some type of emotional pain right now that is creating the desire for change. This is an example of positive pain, and this is pain working for you. Avoiding this positive pain will only cause you more pain in the long run. The pain you suffer from staying the same and not changing is an example of negative pain. A pain that keeps you the same and ultimately leads to more pain is meaningless. The suffering that you go through to change can lead to growth that you never imagined. Avoiding this positive pain keeps you the same. Some people suffer incredible pain from their current circumstances because they are avoiding change. The combination of enduring the negative pain of staying the same, combined with an unspiritual attitude about suffering, leads to misery.

Here's a blatant yet cathartic example from my own life about these two types of pain. Several years ago, there were times in my life when I intentionally decided not to change. Due to this rebellion, I was resisting God, and that always causes pain. In one such situation, my wife conjured great patience and wrote me a lengthy letter to express how badly my pride was hurting her and our relationship. I was aware of the letter, and we decided to set up a time to discuss it. The plan for this discussion was to go to a park about six miles from our house for me to read the letter and respond to it. The letter was eloquently and lovingly written and expressed my wife's concern, hurt, anger, disappointment and fear about my pride. I cannot remember a time prior to that when she was so open and vulnerable. She provided several examples of how my pride was affecting her and our marriage. After I read the letter about my pride, I was far from humble. I crumbled it up, threw it at her, and began the six mile walk home. I was absolutely furious. Since I had mastered the art of making our problems her fault, I took no responsibility for my actions. At this point, I was experiencing a great deal of pain. However, it was the familiar negative pain I had felt hundreds of times before that led me to remain the same. On that long walk home, I felt another strange sort of pain. It was the power of soul-burning and gut-wrenching positive pain. After my anger calmed down, I humbled out and prayed for heavenly guidance to see what I could not see at that time. In that moment, something like metaphorical scales fell from my eyes, and I felt an intense remorse for causing my wife so much hurt. By the time I got home, I was a blubbering and bawling mess but in much less negative pain. My positive pain hurt badly, but we were able to discuss the letter. As a result, I made a much needed breakthrough in my pride. For years before this time, I avoided the positive pain of change that, when embraced, led to my healing. That day was a turning point in my life due to the breakthrough I made in pride. I have had many since then and need more. From times like these, I have learned the healing power of the positive pain of change and the destructive power of the pain that keeps us the same.

In this life, suffering is inevitable, but misery is optional. This phrase may be confusing, but let me explain because this is an important concept to grasp. You may currently be experiencing some sort of physical, emotional, spiritual or psychological suffering. Too many Christians avoid suffering like the plague because they associate suffering with misery. Our attitude about suffering will determine whether we are miserable or not. Seeing the benefits of suffering will help you view pain from another perspective. The latter is the one that God has and wants to pass on to His children.

### Jesus' View of Suffering

Our culture fosters such a prevalent pain avoidance mentality that even the strongest Christians can be tempted to conform to it. Many weaker Christians vow to avoid any type of pain at all costs. This view of even positive pain keeps many Christians from making spiritual breakthroughs.

Avoiding the pain of changing their lives only leads to more pain. We must have a godly view of suffering in order to grow as Christians. We gain this godly view of pain from God's word.

Let me quickly share some Scriptures that address the issue of suffering.

*[Jesus] was despised and rejected by men, a man of sorrows, and familiar with suffering.*
Isaiah 53:3a

*For just as the sufferings of Christ flow over into our lives, so also through Christ our comfort overflows.*
2 Corinthians 1:5

*During the days of Jesus' life on earth, he offered up prayers and petitions with loud cries and tears to the one who could save him from death, and he was heard because of his reverent submission. Although he was a son, he learned obedience from what he suffered.*
Hebrews 5:7-8

Jesus was familiar with suffering and allowed it to work for Him. Do you have the same attitude? I had to make a major attitude adjustment to change my view of suffering. Jesus was not a wimp who avoided pain like I did. If He learned obedience from what He suffered, so can we. He faced emotional pain when sweating drops of blood as He prayed in the Garden of Gethsemane. He endured more emotional pain when all of the disciples deserted Him later that night. He faced spiritual pain when He felt separated from God on the cross. He faced physical pain during a flogging preceding the crucifixion and certainly experienced excruciating pain on the cross. As His disciples, we must also embrace the fact that we will face spiritual, physical, emotional, and psychological pain. As a disciple of Jesus,

His pain will flow over into our lives. The bottom line is that suffering is part of following the Son of God. When we make Jesus Lord of our lives, we also need to embrace His view of suffering.

Paul embraced and adopted the Lord's view of suffering, as evidenced in his discourse on suffering in Romans 5. Here, Paul explains two cycles that occur when we experience suffering. One is spiritual, and one is worldly. The cycle we choose will determine the outcome of our suffering. If we view suffering negatively, we will be tempted to give up and miss the opportunity for change. When we give up, we also lose an opportunity to gain perseverance, and we will ultimately lack the character and hope to make breakthroughs or any difficult changes. Our character then becomes polluted with this quitter's mentality because our tolerance for pain is low. Change, therefore, becomes harder and harder the more we languish rather than forging ahead. Instead of hopeful, we become hopeless. Caught in a downward spiral, we suffer, quit, get worse, become discouraged, and ultimately, lose hope for further attempts to change. Every revolution of this cycle takes us further down a spiral that leads to rock bottom. As you can see, quitting leads to breakdowns, not breakthroughs.

Conversely, we can persevere for positive outcomes and channel our suffering into an upward spiral. In this positive cycle, we gain qualities such as endurance, stronger character and increased hope for further changes. Applying a deeper meaning to your suffering will make a huge difference in how you experience it. If you focus on the pain of the suffering, it is difficult to keep going. The Bible says Jesus focused on the other side of suffering: "for the joy before him [Jesus] endured the cross" (Hebrews 12:2). Jesus understood that on the other side of His suffering there was something better, worth enduring the pain to achieve. We must develop this same approach. You can endure the pain if you see the gain.

What is on the other side of your suffering? If we quit, the result will be more pain. If we persevere, the result will be transformation and hope. By definition, perseverance means that something is difficult; we are tired and feel like giving up. Choosing to persevere leads to breakthroughs. Character is forged in the heat of the fire, not on the periphery. Character and hope are essential qualities for making future breakthroughs. Developing a more spiritual attitude about suffering is essential to making and sustaining the spiritual breakthroughs you seek. The perseverance, character and hope you stand to gain from suffering will not only help you but will also help many others. Just as we benefit from the sufferings of Paul and Jesus, others can benefit from our suffering. Through tales of your prior experience and triumph, you can give someone else hope for change. Paul rejoiced in suffering because he knew the benefits and the outcome of his suffering. Adopting this approach will help you make it through the difficult times on your journey of transformation.

# Chapter 15

# Change Your Attitude about Weaknesses

A core belief I held onto for years was: "weaknesses are *absolutely* unacceptable." In the past, I was completely horrified and even mortified by weaknesses. This core belief was anchored to the deepest part of my soul and very difficult to change. I thought for a long time that I was alone in this core belief. After working with others who suffer from this same misconception, I realized many Christians take a similar view of weakness. Needless to say, we must develop a better attitude about weakness if we are going to make and sustain spiritual breakthroughs.

How do you feel about weaknesses? In the past I have hated, despised, resented, and been ashamed of them. How is that for a positive attitude? Many Christians view weakness in the same manner, if not worse. Since I viewed my weaknesses so negatively, I did not discuss them or address them. Although I thought they were camouflaged and concealed, others saw them clearly. I was embarrassed for these flaws to come into the light, but keeping them to myself bred shame. All of my negativity about these weaknesses caused me a great deal of emotional and spiritual distress. My core belief about weaknesses developed very early. It must have started at birth, since I can remember it from my earliest years. I was raised in a military family and lived at home until I turned 18. I went to college on an ROTC scholarship and served in the military for seven years. By the time I became an adult, I was thoroughly indoctrinated into the military's zero-tolerance view of weakness. In a military battle, any flaws should be covered up, concealed, camouflaged, and kept secret. The enemy wants to discover your vulnerabilities, so they can exploit and use them to defeat you. In the past, I had this same attitude about personal weaknesses.

However, God views imperfections differently. In order to change, I had to let God's thoughts become my thoughts. Would you have ever come to God if you were not weak at some point? We are knit together by God therefore our weaknesses are there for a reason. The apostle Paul also had to drastically change his attitude about weaknesses.

*To keep me from becoming conceited because of these surpassingly great revelations, there was given me a thorn in my flesh, a messenger of Satan, to torment me. Three times I pleaded with the Lord to take it away from me. But he said to me, 'My grace is sufficient for you, for my power is made perfect in weakness.' Therefore I will boast all the more gladly about my weaknesses, so that Christ's power may rest on me. That is why, for Christ's sake, I delight in weaknesses, in insults, in hardships, in persecutions, in difficulties. For when I am weak, then I am strong.*
2 Corinthians 12:7-10

Paul's thorn led him to not just pray but plead with God to take it away. If you are like me, you may feel that you have several thorns, multiple messengers of Satan. At times, there seems to be an army of them. Pride, arrogance, and selfishness are but a few of my personal thorns. Each has its own negative and demonstrative message from Satan, lying, "these weaknesses are too big for God to handle and too difficult for you to breakthrough."

Paul learned to view imperfections as an opportunity for God's power and grace to work in his life. With a lot of prayer, help, work, and practice, I learned to adopt this same core belief about weaknesses. How about you? What if you chose the same attitude? Paul said that when he was weak, he was strong. When I see my weaknesses, the last thing I feel is strong. I feel afraid, anxious, angry, annoyed, and so on. The reason I felt these emotions was because in the past I did not have a godly attitude about weaknesses. God can take them away any time He chooses. Instead, He decides to let us wrestle with them and work through them. It is through these vulnerabilities that God demonstrates His grace and power. Before, Satan used my weaknesses against me. Now, I see that even my weaknesses can work for me by helping me rely more on God and His grace. Paul seemed to have a better understanding of grace than anyone else in the Bible, except for Jesus. Why? One reason may be that he was very aware of his weaknesses. When you can view weaknesses as a way for God to work in your life, you can begin to boast about them as Paul did. I am still working on boasting and delighting in my flaws, but at least I am making progress.

The process of changing our attitude about weakness goes like this: just decide to view weakness differently. Obviously, this is not as simple as I make it seem, but the difference in attitude simply comes by taking a more spiritual view of weaknesses. Once you accept them and view them differently, you will feel differently about them, too. This is part of Paul's secret to being content in all circumstances. My decision to view weaknesses differently was a result of a great deal of praying for a different attitude about them.

I also had to allow God's truth to replace the personal lies I believed about them. My core belief about weaknesses now is that they are acceptable, profitable, and most importantly, changeable. They are a way for God to work through me. In the past, I wanted God to work through my strengths, and thankfully, He has. But God also wants to display His power and glory in uncomfortable ways, like through our weaknesses. I now allow Him the opportunity to do so.

One passage that helped me decide to change my attitude about weakness can be found in Hebrews 11. Towards the end of the chapter, the writer fires off several examples of weak people who God used in a powerful way.

*And what more shall I say? I do not have time to tell about Gideon, Barak, Samson, Jephthah, David, Samuel and the prophets, who through faith conquered kingdoms, administered justice, and gained what was promised; who shut the mouths of lions, quenched the fury of the flames, and escaped the edge of the sword; whose weakness was turned to strength; and who became powerful in battle and routed foreign armies.*
Hebrews 11:32-34

God used all these heroes of faith in spite of their weakness, not because of their strengths. You, too, can claim the promise that weakness can be turned into strength. How is that possible, you ask? Great question. You simply decide to believe God's promise over your unspiritual core beliefs and feelings. God used all of these heroes of faith because they allowed Him to use them in spite of their weaknesses. My weaknesses now serve several good purposes in my life. They help me be more humble. Increased humility helps me to draw closer to God, my wife, my daughters, and other close relationships. They humble me and allow me the opportunity to get help from others. The end result is that I am more spiritual, which leads to being a better husband, father and friend. The decision to change his view of weakness transformed Paul. The decision I made to change this unspiritual core belief radically changed my life, too. Even as a Christian, I conformed to the world's view of character flaws. Thankfully, my mind is being transformed by God's word. As Paul learned to obey God's word, he was transformed from a persecutor to a preacher. Making the same decision about weaknesses can radically transform your life as well.

# Chapter 16

# Failure Is Not Fatal

One of the many problems we face in the spiritual breakthrough process is failure. In spite of our best efforts, we can fall short of our goals, fall back into old sinful behaviors, or relapse. Our attitude toward failure is crucial to the success of future attempts at making breakthroughs. Many Christians have a core belief that "failure is fatal." This core belief was another I held onto with great fervor. The military does not have a very forgiving attitude toward failure. A failed mission is very costly. Failure means that lives and equipment are lost. If we fail a mission, the enemy wins. Success at any cost was often stressed in our pre-mission briefings. This view of failure was not difficult for me to grasp. I hated losing at anything from my earliest memories. For me, failure and losing were absolutely unacceptable.

Many Christians view failure as fatal and stop trying to change. They ask, "Why should I try again if I am just going to fail?" Can you relate to this logic? But who said failure is fatal? Where is that in the Bible? This thought is another example of worldly thinking. God views failure very differently than I do. God sees our failures as an opportunity to extend grace. We often see failure as disgrace. I will use two apostles, Peter and Judas, as examples to explore the outcomes of these two perspectives. Both men failed miserably. Peter flourished, and Judas floundered. We get to choose our response to failure. Our response to failure will have a significant impact upon us spiritually, emotionally and psychologically. Our attitude toward failure can even determine one's will to live and result in an end of life decision.

The Apostle Peter was one of the greatest Biblical "failures" of all time. He lost his faith, his passion and courage, but thankfully, he did not lose his soul. He failed when he walked on water because he gave in to fear when he saw the wind and waves. He failed to see many of the teachings of Jesus on greatness and serving others. The night before the crucifixion, Peter failed Jesus multiple times. In the Garden of Gethsemane, Jesus asked Peter, James, and John to pray for Him in an incredible time of need. Three times, Jesus went off a short distance to pray alone and came back to find them sleeping rather than praying. Later that same night, Peter failed again when he denied the Lord three times. Peter was so adamant in his denial of knowing Jesus that he cursed. Earlier that night at supper, Peter had boasted that he would die with Jesus. Not only did Peter deny Jesus, he disowned Him. Peter wasn't at the cross when Jesus died or at the tomb when Jesus rose from the grave. Peter was on a roll of failure. I can recall discouraging and disheartening times in my life when it seemed like failure awaited me at every turn. In times like these, we can make unspiritual decisions we may regret for a lifetime. In spite of all his failures, Peter did not quit. Why? My conclusion is that Peter believed no matter how badly he failed, Jesus continued to believe in him. This concept is hard for me to grasp, but it is true. How could Jesus forgive Peter for all that failure? The Apostle John records the amazing reinstatement of Peter by Jesus in the last chapter of his gospel. This moving reconciliation can also help you come to believe that Jesus has not lost His vision for you. If Jesus could forgive Peter for his failures, He will do the same for us. Perhaps God allowed Peter to fail so miserably to give us all hope for our own reinstatement someday.

Perhaps Peter's reinstatement inspired him to write this passage years later:

*Humble yourselves, therefore, under God's mighty hand, that he may lift you up in due time. Cast all your anxiety on him because he cares for you. Be self-controlled and alert. Your enemy the devil prowls around like a roaring lion looking for someone to devour. Resist him, standing firm in the faith, because you know that your brothers throughout the world are undergoing the same kind of sufferings. And the God of all grace, who called you to his eternal glory in Christ, after you have suffered a little while, will himself restore you and make you strong, firm and steadfast. To him be the power forever and ever. Amen.*
1 Peter 5:6-11

In spite of his failures, Peter continued to be an apostle. He became a pillar of the early church leadership, and he wrote two books of the New Testament. Maybe Peter accomplished these things because he changed his view of failure. I often wondered how Peter worked through all of his failures and all of the intense emotions connected to them. His victories over failure continue to amaze me. He certainly did not have the "failure is fatal" core belief that I did. The verse above gives me insight into how Peter rebounded from his many missteps.

Imagine the emotional sufferings, including guilt, shame, and humiliation, that Peter went through as a result of his mistakes. Can you relate? I felt each of these emotions intensely after various failures in my life. These emotions can become unbearable, even for Christians. Perhaps all of these intense emotions led Judas to the decision to hang himself. But Peter took a different approach to dealing with his intense emotions. Peter failed for the same reasons we do. He did not follow Jesus' example for dealing with difficult situations. Peter's pride and self-reliance led to disaster just as mine did. Peter, however, learned the value of humbling himself before God. While Peter slept, Jesus gave God His anxiety about going to the cross. Jesus heard the roaring lion yet stood firm because He relied upon God. Peter, on the other hand, heard the roar and ran. Jesus was firmly convinced that God would raise Him from the dead. Peter thought it was nonsense. Through all of these failures, however, Peter came to understand grace.

Peter decided to rely upon God's grace to overcome his feelings about his failures. Do you limit God's ability to extend grace? Have you ever thought your failures were too big for grace to cover? Peter realized that he was called to God's eternal glory, not eternal gloom. Peter perhaps had the biggest pity party of all time after his mistakes. Maybe he recited his résumé of failure over and over as I chose to do at times. Pity parties are for those who do not understand or accept God's grace. We must believe that God's grace can cover any failure. Peter believed he could fail miserably multiple times, and God's grace would still be there. God does not have a grace shortage. God's grace led Peter to the core belief that he could be restored. Peter believed he could be transformed from a miserable failure to a mighty fanatic. Through this metamorphosis, Peter was made into everything he was not during Jesus' last few days on Earth. Peter's lack of courage led him to let down his Lord, Savior and friend, but through grace, he became strong, firm, and steadfast. Any Christian, regardless of the number or severity of your failures, can be restored just like Peter.

If it weren't for Peter's failures, we may not have this Scripture which has encouraged countless people over the past two thousand years. What if Peter quit after any one of those failures? Certainly the course of Biblical history would be dramatically changed. In stark contrast to Peter's example of fruitful failure, the Bible gives us the story of Judas, an example of one such failure who gave up on grace and achieved a very different outcome. Who names their son Judas? There are no churches, religious orders, or books of the Bible named after him. You see where I am going with this.

Judas betrayed Jesus by handing Him over to the Pharisees in exchange for a mere 30 pieces of silver. The story of Judas' death is told in Matthew 27:3-10. Filled with remorse for his actions which resulted in Jesus' condemnation, Judas hung himself.

Both Peter and Judas betrayed their confidence in God, yet Peter was able to make a breakthrough, despite all of the intense emotions associated with his failures. Failure can only be fatal if we allow it. Those humbling moments give God an incredible opportunity to express His grace and love for us. Overcoming your failures can inspire many others to do the same.

The issue you must address is not, "Will I fail?" The answer to that question is a resounding, "Yes!" The question is, "How will I view the failure?" Will you get back up? The failure does not lie in the unsuccessful attempt to change. The failure lies in either not trying to change or not getting back up after an unsuccessful attempt. In spite of all his blunders, Peter did not allow failure to define him. However, he did allow it to refine him.

## Chapter 17

# Playing the Victim and Other Roles

I f you are attempting to make and sustain spiritual break-throughs, you may be going through a difficult time in your life. To better expedite and illuminate your current challenges, I recommend taking a moment to consider the approaches you have used when facing difficult situations in the past. This increased awareness will help you gain insight into the probable outcomes of current and future dilemmas. The best way to predict future performance is to look at the past. If you failed at making spiritual breakthroughs in the past, your approach to adversity may be to blame.

The *role you played* when facing previous challenges will have a tremendous impact on how you experience your current challenges. I am not referring to roles in a movie, like hero or villain, or a role in the family, like the scapegoat. I am talking about a core belief we use to approach difficult situations. The role we choose to play is determined by our core beliefs and how we view ourselves under duress. Below are three examples of core beliefs we may inadvertently or intentionally utilize when facing stressful situations. This discussion can be confusing for some because these approaches are not used at all times and in all circumstances. However, we generally play one of these roles as we approach difficulties. I use examples of people from the Bible, so you can see the results of holding on to these core beliefs.

It may surprise you that we are not always aware of such an important aspect of our lives like a core belief. Previously, I was guided through life by a mindset I could not articulate with an origin I could not define. Some core beliefs are like the wind or the tide. We can see their effect, but we cannot really see the cause. Core beliefs can have a very powerful impact on the direction of our life, but we cannot seem to figure out why life turns out the way it does. It just seems to happen that way, and the mystery goes unsolved. The longer the mystery continues, the worse things can get. I am grateful that God provided me insight into a core belief that guided me early as a Christian. A better understanding helped me to make the changes I needed to pursue the full life Jesus promised.

The mystery of why life turns out the way it does often begins in early childhood. Since we cannot recall not having a particular core belief, we think it has always been there. It is important to identify such core beliefs, so we can change them and stop the destruction they can cause in our lives and the lives of others. We cannot change what we are not aware of. We can approach trials as either a victim, survivor, or thriver. The following discussion on the victim's core belief is provided to make you more cognizant of an approach to difficulty which may be guiding you that you are not fully aware of.

## The Victim

The victim is a person who does not have a full life as a Christian and thinks it is someone else's fault. If you are a victim, the list of those responsible for your lack of fullness may be long or short, but your name is not on it. Perhaps you allowed Satan to steal this abundant life from you by blaming your past. Many Christians are victims of mental, emotional, and even sexual abuse in childhood. It is very easy for those who are victims of any type of abuse as a child to fall back into the victim role even as an adult. The victim role is appropriate in abusive situations from the past. Taking on this role helped you to survive some horrible events. It is easier to accept something bad that happened to you when you realize that whatever happened was not your fault. Victims are powerless over a situation and are not responsible. Embracing these truths and understanding that you were a victim can help you endure the unimaginable.

However, if you were a victim in your past, it can be easy for you to inappropriately apply the core belief that you are a victim even to situations that you can control. If you adopt this core belief in times of difficulty, you may find yourself victimized by a host of other things. Victims can allow emotions, events, and circumstances to dictate their behaviors. The core belief of, "I am victim of my current situation," can keep the individual from taking responsibility for their actions. If you are not responsible for your actions, you do not need to change. If change provokes fear in you, it is easy to slip back into feeling powerless, even in situations you can control. As you can imagine, emerging from the "I am a victim" core belief can be very difficult. Another difficult thing about this mindset is that you may not be conscious of the fact that you are playing the role of the victim. This fact must be presented to you if you are going to change. This information may be met with shock and resistance. The longer you remain the victim to the situation, the longer you will stay the same. Coming out of the victim mindset can be very frightening because it comes with expectations of getting better.

Victims may talk about changing something but do not seem to be able to carry it through. When asked why they were unsuccessful at staying clean or sober, for example, they often make excuses. They may say things like, "I couldn't help it," or, "I couldn't handle the situation without relapsing." For someone with a victim mentality, there always seems to be some person, emotion, or circumstance that is too big and too powerful to overcome. Victims feel powerless and therefore do not take action. However, victims are not powerless. Victims can be empowered to change through God's power.

The victim is also a master at rationalizing why change does not occur. Victims are often content with "trying to change" rather than making a change. The victim is accustomed to and comfortable in failure and has not yet learned to live in success. Victims may even sabotage progress because success is so unfamiliar and uncomfortable. These individuals have a fear of spiritual heights. This self-sabotage is very confusing and frustrating for the people in their lives. The people who care for them do not understand the thinking that deliberately sabotages the progress they make. Victims want circumstances to change rather than changing themselves.

The "I am a victim" core value started long ago. In the Garden of Eden, Adam blamed Eve for his sin; Eve blamed the serpent; and you know the rest of the story. Victims are masters at "The Blame Game." If you are holding on to the "I am a victim" core belief, God wants to empower you to change your approach to life. "I am powerless over people, emotions, circumstances or situations," is another core belief that must change. You must decide that you are not going to allow yourself to be victimized by anyone or anything again. As victims take charge of their lives, they can make radical changes. Jesus did not allow events or circumstances to dictate His behaviors. He does not want His followers to be victims but victors. Take some time and examine whether or not you are allowing yourself to be victimized by circumstances in your life. If so, take charge of your life and allow God to help you make breakthroughs in this area.

## The Survivor

If you are a survivor, you may find it offensive that I consider this a role which needs to change. I know many survivors who are extremely proud of this identity. Allow me to explain why this core belief needs to be addressed. The bottom line is that Jesus did not have a survivor mentality. He does not teach His followers just to survive difficult times but to thrive in spite of trouble. Changing this core belief of being a survivor is also very difficult for some. It was very difficult for me. I was the poster child for surviving solo. This mindset helped me get through many challenges I faced earlier in life. The core belief of the survivor is that life is simply one obstacle or trial after another. Life is to be endured until arrival in heaven. *Then* the "full life" begins. Life for the survivor is an endless parade of difficulties and trials to be endured with the satisfaction that they are still standing but with little joy. Difficulties seem to be their cross to bear.

You can spot a survivor by their vocabulary. When a survivor is asked how they are doing, they respond with phrases like, "I'm still here," "I'm making it," "I'm surviving," "I'm getting by," and so on. The survivor's apparent goal each day is to endure the day rather than enjoy the day. Certainly we all have stressful days we are happy to get through, but the survivor makes this approach a lifestyle. The core belief of a survivor may be healthier and more productive than that of the victim, but God has a higher calling for His children. Survivors often lack joy because they wait in expectation of the next bad thing to come their way. They do not enjoy the fair weather days because they know storms are coming. They are more interested in preparing for the next potential disaster than enjoying the current blessings that God gives them. Survivors need to be revived.

Like the victim, this core belief often develops early in life. Survivors are often raised in a home where getting by was the goal. This mindset and approach to life is generally learned in youth but can be unlearned. If you have this approach to life, it was most likely impressed upon you and eventually formed in you. More awareness of this approach to life can help you change it. There are two types of survivors that deserve more discussion.

**The Dependent Survivor**

A classic example of a dependent survivor is the story of the invalid at the pool of Bethesda in Jerusalem. This man's encounter with Jesus is recorded in John 5. During the time of Jesus, there was a tradition that surrounded this pool. Occasionally, an angel would stir the pool, and the first person in the water was healed. Jesus had an encounter with an invalid and learned that he had been in this condition for 38 years. That is a long time to keep surviving, but somehow this man figured out a way to keep going. This invalid had people in his life who helped him get to the pool when the water stirred. Someone helped him get food, water, clothing, and so forth. Needless to say, he was a very resourceful man. I am sure, at times, he got caught in the rain, stuck in the heat or the cold, and went hungry and thirsty for long periods of time. He had the art of surviving down to a science. The dependent survivor generally has several people in his or her life whose self-imposed duty is to keep this person going. Often the people in the survivor's life are enablers and keep the individual surviving day to day. These people can eventually become very resentful of their duty but learn how to survive their "lot in life." If these worn out people leave, the survivor will recruit others, usually through manipulation, into the supportive role. Enablers generally gravitate to and cling to survivors. Replacing people to help support the survivor is not that difficult.

When Jesus learned that this invalid survived for 38 years, He simply asked the man, "Do you want to get well?" (John 5:6). This question may seem out of place. You may be thinking, "Of course he wants to get well; look at how long he has been trying." But Jesus asked the question for a reason. One would think that after this period of time the invalid would eventually be at the right place at the right time. After 38 years, it is easy to fall into the rut of simply surviving. Jesus had a greater vision for this man, just as He has a greater vision for us than simply surviving. Sadly, many believers are around Jesus for a long time with the same result. They survive life day in and day out. They firmly believe that God helped them make it this far in life and give God the credit for getting them through all of life's difficulties. These Christians, however, are often unaware of the full life they could be living. They are so focused on surviving that they are not aware they can learn to thrive. To their credit, most survivors will not allow themselves to be victimized by anyone or anything. These survivors, however, generally do not make much spiritual progress. Most survivors are just trying to make it through life on a day-to-day basis.

Jesus healed the man at the pool and later saw him at the temple. It seems like Jesus' interest in his life led the man to a better spiritual place. Jesus performed a miracle in this man's life, and he can do the same for us. Jesus called him to get up and walk for the first time in 38 years. The invalid had a plan to be healed that did not work. Jesus had a better plan. The man obeyed and was healed. Will you obey Jesus when he calls you to do something you have been unable to do in a long time? Or maybe have never done at all? Remember, Jesus believes that change is possible. Your core belief for how you approach difficulties will make all the difference in the outcome of your life. Stop surviving and let Jesus teach you how to thrive.

## The Solo Survivor

There is also another type of survivor. The demon-possessed man, named Legion, who Jesus encountered in Mark 5, is an example of what I call the "solo survivor." This man was banned from the town and lived among the tombs. The Bible says he was often chained by hand and foot. You can imagine his trust issues with others. His limited interactions with people consisted of being banished or bound up by them. Legion had to figure out a way to survive life on his own. He was socially ostracized and survived by his own wits. Unlike dependent survivors, the independent variety accepts very little support from others. Due to trust issues or other concerns, they rely upon their own strength and skills to make it through their trials. These individuals often do not feel like they "fit in." They may attend church but are not involved and may be perceived as "loners." A core belief of the solo survivor is often that others cannot be trusted and will hurt them. This type of survivor will gladly share with others how they survived the past trials solo with great detail. They will also look into their crystal ball and say more trails are coming which they will face alone, too. The independent survivor's focus is on their trials. They are often unaware of the full life they could be living. They overflow with satisfaction but lack serenity. Jesus wants to heal their hurt and teach them about the full life they can have in Him.

Legion was healed that day by his encounter with Jesus. He ran up to Jesus, fell on His knees and shouted at the top of his voice for help. This scene must have been very intimidating for the disciples to watch. This man's life was totally out of control. You may feel that your life is out of control as well. Legion had what I call the "gift of desperation." This gift will lead us to do whatever it takes to change, even if it means trusting others. Making spiritual breakthroughs, at times, will call for desperation. My biggest breakthroughs came at my most desperate times. Making these breakthroughs required me to give up the core belief that "I cannot trust God or others." In spite of Legion's bad experiences with others, he decided to trust God. Jesus responded to this man's desperation, and He will respond to yours. Do you have the gift of desperation? Are you willing to start trusting Jesus to release you from your chains? Jesus is calling you today to stop settling for just surviving and start thriving. The Apostle Paul is an amazing example of someone who could have settled for surviving but chose to thrive instead.

**The Thriver**

Thankfully, there is third way to approach life, a role I refer to as "the thriver." The word thrive simply means to prosper vigorously. A thriver is not a victim of circumstances, emotions, the past, or a host of other things. The thriver is not interested in just *going* through trials but *growing* through them as well. The Apostle Paul is an excellent example of a thriver. He went through incredible events such as being stoned (with rocks not drugs), flogged, persecuted, exposed to death, put in prison, beaten with rods, and shipwrecked, to name a few. Many of the events he endured are recorded in the book of Acts and 2 Corinthians 11. In spite of all of these situations, Paul maintained a positive attitude.

*Therefore we do not lose heart. Though outwardly we are wasting away, yet inwardly we are being renewed day by day. For our light and momentary troubles are achieving for us an eternal glory that far outweighs them all.*
2 Corinthians 4:16-17

A thriver is able to put problems in perspective. Paul considered his problems "light and momentary." He could view difficulties in this manner because he was able to put his problems into an eternal perspective. Paul did not have any magical apostle powers that enabled him to effortlessly adopt this approach to life. He had to *choose* the core belief of thriving and *learn* this approach to facing life's difficulties. He learned it from Jesus and others. Paul's problems were light because he gave them to God. Here is another example of Paul's core belief of being a thriver:

*We do not want you to be uninformed, brothers, about the hardships we suffered in the province of Asia. We were under great pressure, far beyond our ability to endure, so that we despaired even of life. Indeed, in our hearts we felt the sentence of death. But this happened that we might not rely on ourselves but on God, who raises the dead.*
2 Corinthians 1:8-9

Paul's core belief was, "I can't, but God can." All of our problems are light and momentary when we put them into an eternal perspective and into God's hands. Paul viewed difficulties as a way to become more God-reliant and less self-reliant. The self-reliant soul cannot thrive. Only those who depend upon God and others can take this approach to life. Adopting this belief revolutionized my view of difficulties. It can be exciting to face difficulties now because I trust God to work things out. Regardless of how events unfold, I know I can emerge from hardship closer to God and more reliant upon Him.

The role we take as we face challenges is crucial to the outcome of the trial. In order to thrive like Paul, we need to change our unspiritual core beliefs. Paul did not want to be victimized by his circumstances or just survive them. He decided to learn and grow from them. Paul's difficulties helped transform him more into the likeness of Christ. Is that your attitude? This world and the church both need many more thrivers. Allow God to empower you as He did Paul and others to adopt the core belief that you, too, can become a thriver.

## Chapter 18

# Change Your View of You

෧

The end result of the unspiritual core beliefs discussed thus far can be a very negative self-image. Sadly, many Christians suffer from low self-esteem. Psychology defines this term to mean an individual's appraisal of their value or worth. There are many reasons for poor self-esteem. It can stem from the individual's upbringing and from making multiple poor decisions. One way to improve self-esteem is to change your view of you. In order to change this view, you will need to begin to see yourself through God's eyes. Once you see yourself from another perspective, you can feel very differently about yourself. The difficulty with this approach is that many Christians also have poor "God-esteem." In other words, because they view themselves in a negative manner, they believe that God views them in the same way. The basis of poor self-esteem is often a core belief that goes something like this: "I am inadequate," "I do not measure up," "I am not good enough," or "I am deficient." You may wonder how these core beliefs develop. Often, these negative core beliefs are a direct result of allowing yourself to be defined by an unhealthy person or a negative event. But God defines you very differently.

If you were raised in a dysfunctional family, you may have one or more of these core beliefs just mentioned. In many cases, these core beliefs continue to develop because as adults we still allow the unhealthy person who originally defined us in these terms to continue to define us in this manner. This unhealthy person may have used verbal abuse to lead you to the conclusion that you are of little or no value. You may be projecting your parent's view of you on to God. In other words, if a parent thought you were worthless, you may project that thought upon God. Since the parent thought you were inadequate, you now believe God thinks you are, too. Regardless of the cause of the negative core belief, the solution is the same. We must allow God to define us. God does not use these negative descriptions mentioned above to describe His children. However, even as Christians and adults we can continue to embrace these negative core beliefs and even cling to them. For some, it is the only identity they have ever known, and this identity, although damaging, can be very difficult to change.

Read how God created you:

*For you created my inmost being; you knit me together in my mother's womb. I praise you because I am fearfully and wonderfully made; your works are wonderful, I know that full well.*
Psalm 139:13-14

God knits us together just as He wants us. In part, we are knit together with strengths. These strengths are knitted in you just like your physical attributes. I am a devout non-knitter, but I have observed it several times. My mother-in-law knitted both of my daughters a baby blanket before they were born. As I watched her work, I could see love in every labor-intensive stitch. The Holy Spirit could have used lots of phrases other than "knit together" to describe the process of our creation. For example, "thrown together" just does not have the same ring to it. Knitting takes a lot of thought, skill and planning. God knit you together with strengths. You will need to identify, validate, and use them to fulfill the unique plan and purpose that God has for your life.

We are not only knit together with strengths and unique traits, but also weaknesses. Does one or both of the words, weakness or strength, make you uncomfortable? Did you speed up a little there in your reading? Did you find yourself wanting to skip that part? That may be part of the problem. Many people find it uncomfortable to talk about one or both of them. Romans 12:3 states that we must view ourselves with sober judgment. Sober means we have an honest view of ourselves that is not too high or too low. We must understand that God gave us our strengths to serve Him and help others. He also gave us our weaknesses, so Christ's power can work through us (2 Corinthians 12:9). God also states that by faith weakness can be turned to strengths (Hebrews 11:34). As Christians, even our weakness can work for us.

Many Christians, especially those with low self-esteem, minimize their strengths and maximize their weaknesses. This approach severely hinders the change process. This distorted view of yourself is neither humble nor accurate. One reason many Christians can have low self-esteem is because their strengths are focused in a negative direction. For example, the Apostle Paul was an extreme man. I consider the quality of being extreme to be a strength. Prior to becoming a Christian, he was extremely opposed to the church. After becoming a Christian, he was extremely dedicated to making disciples. In his case, the strength was originally channeled in a negative direction. After his conversion, he took this strength, focused it on God, and the rest is history. Just because your strengths are not working for you now does not mean you don't have strengths.

Did you take the time to make a list of your strengths, as recommended earlier in the book? Get others who know you well to make a list, too. Compare your list with others. The people in your life who know you well have a panoramic 360 degree view of you. If they are supportive, they will not be focused on your weaknesses like you are. It may be difficult for you to get your focus off of your weaknesses for a while, but do it anyway. Focusing on your weaknesses is only exacerbating your problems. Sadly, many believers do not feel that they are worthy of change because they have such a poor view of themselves. This fresh and more accurate perspective will help you to move forward in making the spiritual breakthroughs you desire.

The same Being who created everything around you and all of the heavenly hosts created you. We are designed and created by the creator of the universe. Genesis 1:27 says we were made in His image. According to Psalm 17:8, we are the apple of His eye. Isaiah 49:16 states that God engraved His people on the palms of His hands. You know you are loved when someone tattoos your name on a body part. God is crazy in love with you like a parent is with a newborn. Even when we disappoint Him, He still loves us. Once these truths sink in, spiritual breakthroughs are bound to happen. In order to make and sustain breakthroughs, you will need to view you the way that God *really* views you. Not the way you think He does. I understand that you may feel this concept is new and difficult, but understand if you don't, you are arguing with the Creator of the universe. Your feelings do not override God's facts. It is very difficult to make breakthroughs with a negative view of yourself. It may take more than this brief discussion to change your view of you, but you need to start somewhere. You are more than the sum of your past mistakes and the problems you may cause. Viewing yourself as the valuable and wonderful creation of God that you are will help you through the transformation process. Embrace God's view of you. Let God define you as a person and not the unhealthy people in your life. In spite of whatever your faults may be, you can change by the power of the Almighty God who made you and loves you.

## Your Decision

As you can imagine, changing core beliefs is a difficult but very necessary step required to make and sustain spiritual breakthroughs. I often tried to change without really believing God's promises. Although the Bible is a book of promises, I have neglected to know them or claim them too many times. The promises of God can become your core beliefs if you work at it. Jesus had these core beliefs and passed them on so His followers could think this way. Your negative feelings about God's promises do not invalidate them, but they will make them untrue for you. Your negative emotions about the promises will also make change more difficult. Your past failures do not invalidate His promises. The same God who promises you salvation and heaven also promises that you can change. Paul said, "For no matter how many promises God has made, they are 'Yes' in Christ" (2 Corinthians 1:20). The same God who transformed Peter, James and Paul can also help you make spiritual breakthroughs if you adopt God's way of thinking. The mindset with which we approach spiritual breakthroughs is paramount. Many Christians believe His promises of victory are true for others but not for themselves. In order to embrace the truth of the promises of God, we must make fundamental changes in our way of thinking.

As I stated earlier, the place to begin the process of change is in the mind. We cannot be transformed into the likeness of Jesus if we do not think like Him. We must come to believe that Jesus always has a greater vision for our lives than the world does. Jesus also empowers us to achieve the impossible. In order to achieve the impossible, we must begin to view life as God intended it to be. In order to change our thoughts, we must adopt His thoughts. Our core beliefs must become God's core beliefs. Once we begin to think more like God, we will see amazing things occur in our lives. We must come to believe that we can change even the seemingly impossible. Decide today to make God's promises your core beliefs.

Now is a good time to "check-in" with how you are doing emotionally. Checking in is the clinical way of identifying your feelings about what you have read thus far. Staying in-tune emotionally is very important. Sometimes emotions are the invisible intangibles that keep us from moving forward. At this point, you may be bombarded and overwhelmed by thoughts like, "look at how much my thinking needs to change!" This response is common because many readers do not purchase books like this to change their thinking. They are not even aware that their way of thinking needs to be different. They often take on pursuits like changing behaviors without being fully aware of all of the negative core beliefs that predisposition them for failure. Others of you may be discouraged by your lack of spiritual progress. The following chapters are designed to provide you with the hope you need to move forward and face your fears of changing any thoughts, feelings, or behaviors that may be holding you back spiritually. The hope you gain from these chapters will propel you forward as you continue your exciting and rewarding journey of transformation.

# PART III

# HOPE

## Chapter 19

# Choose Hope

*During the fourth watch of the night Jesus went out to them, walking on the lake. When the disciples saw him walking on the lake, they were terrified. "It's a ghost," they said, and cried out in fear. But Jesus immediately said to them: "Take courage! It is I. Don't be afraid."*
Matthew 14:25-27

Think about the situation the disciples are enduring in Matthew 14:27 when Jesus tells them, *"Don't be afraid."* The night is very dark; there is a strong wind; and someone is walking on the water. The ship could have succumbed to the waves at any moment, and they all could have drowned. I remember reading this verse and asking myself, "Is it possible *not* to be afraid in a situation like this?" Terror seems like a very appropriate response to this occasion, for these circumstances all seem like pretty good reasons to be terrified, anxious or overwhelmed. In this story Peter shows us by example the type of spiritual heights we can obtain when we *choose* not to be controlled by our emotions. Moments later, Peter also demonstrates what happens when we *allow* our emotions to take over. Giving in to emotions caused Peter to sink. Giving in to our emotions causes us to sink spiritually, too. Our emotions, however, only have the power that we *choose* to grant them. I have learned, if I view the world as Jesus did, I can *choose* not to be controlled by emotions. We can always *choose* hope over our feelings, regardless of the strength of the storm.

The field of psychology has conducted much research on what helps people recover from any type of physical, emotional, financial, medical, or mental health condition. You may immediately think that the most helpful thing is medication or some type of therapy. Both of these interventions are very important, but neither is most important. Regardless of the condition or situation, the number one reason people improve is *hope*. Hope is a feeling but also a choice, an incredibly empowering choice that can radically change your life if you allow it.

Even after becoming a Christian, I did not think I had a choice but to obey my emotions. You may know from experience that this is a scary way to live. I could not predict how I was going to act because I did not know how I was going to feel. I lived that way for years prior to becoming a Christian and saw no hope for change. Whenever an intense emotion came, I did not believe there was another choice I could make. Jesus taught His disciples a better way to live. Each day, I have a choice to make, to obey my emotions or obey God. I now choose hope over my negative emotions, like fear, and believe it is a better way to live. Allowing change can be a terrifying choice, but you will need to make that choice in order to make spiritual breakthroughs. In order to allow change, you will need hope. Change does not magically happen or come to you; you must go to it. Once you allow yourself the opportunity to change, God and others can provide you all the hope you will need.

Were you surprised to learn that hope is the *most* important thing that helps people improve? Hopelessness about life or circumstances causes people to give up trying. Many believers stop really living and settle for merely existing because they have lost hope for change. Sadly, many of these believers conclude that they cannot overcome their obstacles and live an abundant life. You may be one of them. Choosing hope is incredibly empowering. Losing hope can result in unthinkable decisions with dire consequences. Each year, approximately 500,000 people in the United States attempt to take their life. Most make this decision as a result of hopelessness. Sadly, approximately 35,000 of them are successful. Suicide is the third leading cause of death among adolescents and young adults. Approximately three people per hour in this country take their own life. Thousands of these souls who attempt suicide consider themselves to be people of faith. I've counseled many believers who have attempted suicide or seriously considered it. I have also counseled some who were eventually successful. Needless to say, the devastation of this decision can last a lifetime for the loved ones left behind. A situation may be challenging, difficult, and even chronic, but it does not need to be hopeless. Suicide is a permanent solution to a temporary problem. Hope, however, is a choice that one can make regardless of the situation.

## Put Your Hope in God

*Find rest, O my soul, in God alone,*
  *my hope comes from him.*
*He alone is my rock and my salvation;*
  *he is my fortress, I will not be shaken.*
Psalm 62:5-6

When people of faith have hope, sometimes their hope is placed in something or someone else other than God. For example, I am blessed to have the opportunity to work with some great physicians who are very skilled in their trade, helping people improve and live a better quality of life. But it's important to remember they are still human. It is very tempting to put hope in people, and many Christians make this mistake. A physician may be great, but none can compare with The Great Physician. In order for hope to be effective, it must have an object. So where have you placed your hope? If you are trying to lose weight, your hope may be in the newest diet. You may be trying to win the lottery in order to change your financial situation, and your hope is in a lucky number. If you suffer from depression, your hope may be in the human hands of a counselor or psychiatrist, or in a bottle of medication. You may have your hope placed in this book or your church. Hope from any source can be helpful. However, placing your hope in God will ultimately lead to your deliverance. Throughout the Old Testament, God warned His people not to place their hope in anything but Him, and we, too, need to heed this warning. Hoping in worldly interventions to make spiritual breakthroughs can be very disappointing and even devastating. Casting Crowns, a contemporary Christian band, wrote a moving and impactful song about hope, titled "Every Man." Visit my web site www.mtccounseling.com for a link to hear this encouraging and applicable song.

## Living Hope

One of the many awesome things about being a Christian is that we can *choose* to have hope regardless of the situation. In 1 Peter 1, Peter writes:

*Praise be to the God and Father of our Lord Jesus Christ! In his great mercy he has given us new birth into a living hope through the resurrection of Jesus Christ from the dead.*
I Peter 1:3

Is your hope alive? For Peter, this living hope was real because of Christ's resurrection. This hope led Peter to do some amazing things throughout the book of Acts. In Acts 2, he preaches the following and speaks about the resurrection on the Day of Pentecost, and over 3,000 souls respond:

*But God raised him from the dead, freeing him from the agony of death, because it was impossible for death to keep its hold on him.*
Acts 2:24

*God has raised this Jesus to life, and we are all witnesses of the fact.*
Acts 2:32

Living hope inspired Peter to preach boldly and to radically change his life. This living hope transformed Peter from a fisherman to a fisher of men and from someone who denied Christ to a dedicated disciple. Think of how hopeless Peter must have felt during the time of the crucifixion of Jesus. Imagine how that feeling changed when the women who encountered Jesus the morning of His Resurrection came back and reported that Jesus' tomb was empty. Luke records that Peter *ran* to the tomb to investigate the event (Luke 24:12). Hope was living inside of Peter, perhaps deep inside, but he found it. Living hope dwells in every Christian. I pray this section on hope will resurrect the hope that lives in you. Hope in God also renews our strength and allows us to not only walk and run again, but also to soar.

The prophet Isaiah wrote:

*...but those who hope in the LORD will renew their strength. They will soar on wings like eagles; they will run and not grow weary, they will walk and not be faint.*
Isaiah 40:31

Have you ever seen an eagle soar? It is a beautiful sight. The eagle locates a pocket of warm air rising, spreads its wings, and lets God, who makes the air rise in the first place, do the rest. Eagles make soaring seem effortless, but they don't begin flight training with this same graceful glide. Undergoing many days of struggle, an eagle must gradually learn the dynamics of flight before mastering it with artful agility. If your hope is in God, you, too, can learn to soar. Do you know someone who makes living an abundant life look easy? They seem to wake up, take off, and let God do the rest. While the rest of us are crashing and burning, they are soaring over the canyons. Your days of soaring will come if you stick with the process of change. Remember, making spiritual breakthroughs is a process that takes time. Capture in your mind the moments that you do soar, and allow them to inspire you to continue on your journey to learn these skills on a regular basis. Hope leads to spiritual soaring. Fear leads to spiritual sinking. We get to make the choice. Allow yourself to have the hope you need to make the spiritual breakthroughs you desire, so you, too, can inspire others.

## Chapter 20

# The God of Hope

❧

### A Small God Provides Little Hope

Your amount of hope will be determined by the size of your God. Let me explain. I counsel many people in involved in various 12 Step Programs, where participants must identify a "higher power" to work the program. This higher power is the one that the individual comes to believe in at Step Two. At Step Three, the individual decides to turn their life and will over to "the god of their understanding." During the course of a person's therapy, I get the opportunity to facilitate many discussions about higher powers. Some choose an inanimate object to be their higher power, while others choose nature or a host of other things. Amazingly, some even choose themselves as their own higher power. It sounds crazy, but I have done it. There have been plenty of times that I put my hope in myself rather than God. If you are honest with yourself, you have, too. Perhaps this self-reliance is preventing you from making spiritual break-throughs. Choosing to put yourself, another person, a program, a church or any other organization over the God of creation as a higher power will not work, like choosing an

AAA battery over a nuclear power plant. So, how big is your God? The size of our problems and the size of our hope are both directly proportional to the size of our God. There is unlimited hope in an infinite God.

Remember the earlier discussion on how awesome God is? I will elaborate further on the power of God later. For now, read the below Psalm and ponder how great and powerful God is:

*By the word of the LORD were the heavens made,*
*their starry host by the breath of his mouth.*
*He gathers the waters of the sea into jars;*
*he puts the deep into storehouses.*
*Let all the earth fear the LORD;*
*let all the people of the world revere him.*
*For he spoke, and it came to be;*
*he commanded, and it stood firm.*
*The LORD foils the plans of the nations;*
*he thwarts the purposes of the peoples.*
*But the plans of the LORD stand firm forever,*
*the purposes of his heart through all generations.*

*We wait in hope for the LORD;*
*he is our help and our shield.*
*In him our hearts rejoice,*
*for we trust in his holy name.*
*May your unfailing love rest upon us, O LORD,*
*even as we put our hope in you.*
Psalm 33:6-11, 20-22

The incredibly powerful God spoke the millions of stars you can see into existence. He also created the billions you cannot see and the rest of the heavens. God made everything out of nothing. His words made it all happen. All of creation was part of God's plan. This same God has a plan for you and your life. He demonstrates His power to you daily through nature and the course of human events. His power is at our command. You tap into that power by putting your hope in Him. Once you begin to get your mind around how amazing God is, you will trust Him more. Trusting His promises over your fears is crucial to making spiritual breakthroughs.

*May the God of hope fill you with all joy and peace as you trust in him, so that you may overflow with hope by the power of the Holy Spirit.*
Romans 15:13

Think about this verse. Not only does God say that you can have hope, He says you can overflow with hope. Overflowing means you have enough for you and for others. Earlier in the book when this verse was quoted, you may have been struggling with the concept of having any hope at all, but God says you can overflow with hope. How does that happen? One way to be filled with abundant hope is to find Biblical characters who struggled and were victorious. Peter is used as an example, above, of someone who regained his hope, and there are many other examples in the Bible.

*For everything that was written in the past was written to teach us, so that through endurance and the encouragement of the Scriptures we might have hope.*
Romans 15:4

Think about the statement, "everything that was written in the past." Paul is speaking specifically about the Old Testament. It is full of amazing examples of hope that surely helped him have hope in his times of need. Hebrews 11 is full of examples of "heroes of faith." These men and women are also examples of "heroes of hope." Let their victories give you hope to make the breakthroughs you desire.

## Against All Hope

Many of the amazing men and women from Hebrews 11 are heroes of hope, but I will focus on Abraham and his wife Sarah. The promise of a child, oddly enough, came when Abraham was at the ripe young age of 75, and Sarah was 65. This is the stage in life when couples generally become grandparents, but for this couple, the promise was a first-born child. They waited 25 years for their promised son, Isaac. In spite of being "as good as dead" (Hebrews 11:12), Abraham put his hope in "the God who gives life to the dead and calls things that are not as though they were" (Romans 4:17). Because he put his hope in God, the Bible has this to say about Abraham:

*Against all hope, Abraham in hope believed and so became the father of many nations.*
Romans 4:18a

Abraham simply *chose* to be hopeful in spite of his circumstances. Imagine going month after month for 24 years without the promise of conception coming true. It is difficult to comprehend how hopeless they could have felt at times. If Abraham and Sarah gave in to discouragement, there would have been no Isaac. The hope you and I gain from their experience would not exist. However, they did choose hope over fear because Abraham chose to believe the God of the universe over his feelings. God has this to say about Abraham and Sarah:

*By faith Abraham, even though he was past age—and Sarah herself was barren—was enabled to become a father because he considered him faithful who had made the promise. And so from this one man, and he as good as dead, came descendants as numerous as the stars in the sky and as countless as the sand on the seashore.*
Hebrews 11:11-12

If you daily choose hope, you will not lose hope. Choosing hope will lead you to be a hero of hope to others. If you lose hope, you will not change or be able to help others change. The hope you find to make spiritual break-throughs can, in turn, inspire countless others to change as well. The patriarch Abraham could hope against worldly reasoning because his hope was in the God who keeps His promises. Some have little hope in God because, frankly, they have a little god. Some people have spiritual dyslexia. I still struggle with it sometimes. What I mean is that I read a verse backwards. I created God in my image whereas the Scriptures state that we are created in His image. The bigger your God, the more hope you will have.

When Abraham struggled with God's promises, God told him to go look at the stars. On a clear night in the desert where Abraham lived, he could see millions of stars. So if you are a quart low on hope, perhaps you have shrunk God down to your size. Take a look at the vast expanse of stars in the sky and ponder your Heavenly Father who created the universe. The bigger you allow God to be, the more hope you will have.

Perhaps you are in a different place spiritually, mentally, and emotionally regarding your attitude about change. You are not hopeless and have decided you are not going to settle for being the same. You will no longer settle for "the same old thing." As we say in 12 Step Programs, you are "sick and tired of being sick and tired." You may have even tried a host of interventions like counseling, medication, prayer, fasting, a psychic reading, a support group, a self-help book, Internet research, advice from friends, prayer, and advice from a guru in the Himalayas, yet nothing has worked. Believe it or not, there is still hope. Wipe the tears of anger and frustration away, take a deep breath, and keep reading. Just because you *feel* like you have tried everything, does not mean there is not another way. Maybe you did not even want to pick up this book, in fear of trying yet again to fail miserably, or so you thought. The fact that you are still trying says something about you; you have what it takes to make that breakthrough you have longed for. You just need some hope to spark the fire of strength within you. Renewed hope will give you the courage to keep trying.

**Hope Busters**

As you can see in the Bible, God has much to say about hope; it is the air that gives our transformation breath and life. Hope allows us to soar like eagles. A lack of hope will cause us to walk like turkeys. Surely by now you are more hopeful. However, many get stuck in emotions that steal our hope. In order to make spiritual breakthroughs, we all must face what I term "hope busters." Here I will address the major ones like fear, guilt, shame, and discouragement. I will confront these emotions with scriptures to demonstrate that we can choose hope over even the most difficult of emotions. There are many emotions that can damage and destroy our hope. It is important in your journey with Jesus to identify these emotions and deal with them in a spiritual manner. King Solomon is famous for his saying, "there is nothing new under the sun" (Ecclesiastes 1:9). There is no feeling you are facing now that someone does not address and overcome in the Bible. God's word can help you deal with any and every negative emotion that is holding you back from making spiritual breakthroughs.

## Chapter 21

# Fear

If you remember, I addressed fear in a previous chapter. There is much to say about this powerful emotion, so I have sprinkled various thoughts about fear throughout the book. Fear is your foe, and like an evil villain in a novel or movie, it will continue to reappear. The apostles were constantly in situations where they had to confront and work through their fears. It seems like almost daily there is a new thing I face that I am afraid to do. In order to make spiritual breakthroughs, we must become familiar and more comfortable with facing fear. My experiences in the military helped me confront major fears. You may be thinking that all fears are major, but some are bigger than others. This training helped me get more comfortable in any distressful situation. Let me share how I was trained to find the courage to leap from an airplane while in airborne school. The same principles will also help you as they have helped me.

Jumping from a plane at combat altitude of 1,000 feet is terrifying for anyone, even those who train others to do so. We often made these jumps at night, with full equipment that could weigh 50 or more pounds. The hull of that plane heard more whispered prayers than most churches. Many things can go wrong during an airborne operation, resulting in injury or death. The ability to address these scary conditions without giving in to fear helps keep the airborne trooper alive. Giving in to fear leads to panic which sends the Christian soldier hurtling towards spiritual disaster.

When I attended the U.S. Army Airborne School, it included three weeks of intense jump training. The first week was called "Ground Week" and taught soldiers to follow orders *exactly*. This principle is very important, and I will expound on it shortly. We also did a lot of physical conditioning, learned how to guide the parachute, and learned how to land. We spent hours exercising and practicing Parachute Landing Falls (PLFs). It may surprise you, but one of the scariest things about jumping is the landing. Becoming proficient at certain skills gave us confidence that we would land safely. Our motto was, "any jump you can walk away from is a good jump." We became very proficient at PLFs, so we could have "good jumps." We did this by jumping from four-foot platforms into sawdust. It is interesting to note that in order to accomplish the ultimate goal of jumping from 1,000 feet, we started at four feet. None of my real jumps were from four feet or into sawdust, but this approach eased us into the real thing. "Balls of the feet, calves, thighs, butt, lats," I heard this phrase a million times. These are the body parts that should hit the ground – in that order. This technique was drilled into our heads, and we practiced PLFs over and over again each day for several hours. The method was so ingrained, I felt like I could execute a PLF coming straight out of a coma.

In the first week of school, we didn't face our ultimate fear of jumping from a plane. Actually, the scariest part of the first week was the relentless correction from the instructors we referred to as "Black Hats." They would yell at us about the smallest imperfections, but they were preparing us for the formidable adventures in the weeks that followed.

We built up confidence in basic skills by doing *exactly* what we were taught by the Black Hats, the experienced para-troopers who, each with hundreds of jumps of experience, assured us that if we followed their instructions, we would earn the coveted paratrooper badge called "jump wings." We knew they each, in turn, had faced their fears, followed the teachings of their instructors, and gained their wings. These shared stories of past experience and success gave us hope that if we did the same, we would also receive our jump wings.

Hebrews 12:2 states Jesus is the "author and perfecter of our faith." He is our pioneer, the one who has gone before us in faith, and He is also our captain. If we take our orders from Him, we will be safe. He orders us not to be afraid. If we allow Him to train and prepare us for fearful situations, we will be successful. Also, it helps to have spiri-tual "Black Hats" in your life, men and women who faced fears and overcame them. I enjoy the wise counsel and encouragement from friends in my life who have hundreds of tales of victories, choosing hope over fear. These souls are invaluable. Learn from them and how they faced their fears, so you can face yours.

The second week was "Tower Week," and it forced us to face our fear of heights. The first tower was 34 feet high. Strapped into a harness attached to a zip line cable, we jumped from the tower and sailed about 50 yards horizon-tally before release. Then, we ran back to the platform and up three stories to strap in again for another jump from the tower. We practiced "exiting the aircraft" again and again because a poor exit can cause the individual to hit the side of the plane. It surprised me how frightening it was to jump from the tower strapped into a harness. My mind reasoned that there was no way to get hurt practicing this procedure. My heart, however, pounded with a different response. It would race as if I had just done sprints. This natural instinct tends to kick in when jumping from high elevations, so we practiced this drill over and over until we were comfortable with the height and form of the maneuver. All we knew about jumping at this point was how to have a good exit, guide the parachute, have a good landing, and do *exactly* what we were told by the trainers.

The thought of making a real jump at this point was still terrifying. I was gaining confidence but not enough to leap from a moving airplane. I did, however, have enough confidence to move into the next phase of training. Perhaps you are at this point in facing your fearful situation. Maybe you are still too fearful to reach your ultimate goal, but there may be a step you can take to keep moving forward in the process of change. It is very important to keep moving forward. Facing the smaller tower now will give you confidence to take on the higher tower later.

The next tower was 250 feet high; I remember seeing these ominous towers the first time I entered the airborne training center in Fort Benning, Georgia. At that time, I was terrified at the thought of attempting this task. However, when the time came to actually perform this part of the training, my panic was at a manageable level. Prior experience had prepared me to face this daunting task. Training on the bigger tower consisted of attaching our opened parachute to a huge metal ring and slowly raising it to the top of the tower. I remember my heart beating like a drum during that slow rise to the top. Once at the top of the tower, the parachute was released from the ring, and we floated down. This exciting part of the training gave us a feeling of what it was like to fall from the sky. We landed in a nice plowed-up field that helped us to land softly. This experience was far less extreme than a real jump, but it gave me the confidence to move forward. My mind reasoned, "the Black Hats told me that if I can do what is necessary at 34 feet, then I can do what is necessary at 250 feet. Therefore, I can do what is necessary for the real thing." Now, use this same line of reasoning for your situation. By this point, you have faced many fears in your life. Do you remember learning how to swim? I nearly drowned but faced the fear and now have many wonderful memories of swimming. Do you remember learning to ride a bike? I wrecked multiple times initially but pushed through the fear. Do you remember taking your first driver's license exam? If you hadn't faced that fear, you would not have your license today. I think you get the point. We have faced many fears in our lives up to this point and lived to tell about it. All of these events were your small platforms. You have faced other fears in your life, too, that represent your towers. Now, let the victory of those fears give you the confidence to face your bigger fears. It's time to make the jump.

The final week of jump school culminates in actually jumping from the plane, a thrilling yet simultaneously terrifying experience. In order to earn airborne wings, we had to make five jumps. Each has its own story and its own personal victory over fear. By this point in the training, we knew all the things that could possibly go wrong during the jump and how to address them. These safety drills were ingrained in us just like the PLFs. The fear that gripped me three weeks prior was no longer impairing me. I learned to let the fear work for me. Fear will paralyze or prepare, so I decided to channel the fear into keeping me focused on that task at hand. I was taught to take an "expect the best but prepare for the worst" approach. When facing difficult situations, many Christians take the opposite approach. When facing a fear, they expect the worst possible thing to happen. During jump school, we fully expected each jump to be safe, but we were prepared for worst-case scenarios. Many Christians remain stuck because they are unprepared to face fear. They feel that fear is an emotion to obey, but we can train ourselves to obey Jesus instead of our fears. Consistently succumbing to fear can cause significant spiritual and psychological damage. Once we begin to give in to the emotion, our world becomes smaller and smaller. The secret is to feel the fear and move forward anyway. That, by definition, is courage.

Giving in to fear is like a cancer that takes over. Once we give into fear, we can choose to take fewer risks and long deeply for comfort and safety. Yielding to fear can also lead to depression, anxiety, low self-esteem and a host of other psychological disorders. In severe cases, it can lead to a debilitating disorder called agoraphobia. People suffering with this condition are so afraid of everything they become confined to their home. Jesus told his disciples not to be afraid on many occasions, even in terrifying situations; the Bible contains many examples of Jesus rebuking cowardly disciples. One such tale is recorded in Matthew 8 when Jesus and the twelve were stuck in a boat during a furious storm. The disciples thought they were going to drown and cried out to Jesus. He told them not to be afraid. Jesus expects us to face our fears, regardless the size of the storm. What storms are terrorizing you? What fears are you falling victim to? You cannot continually give in to fear and expect to make spiritual breakthroughs.

As discussed at the very beginning of this section about hope, Matthew 14 records an amazing spiritual break-through. One windy night, Jesus walked on water towards the disciples in a boat, and they "cried out in fear" (Matthew 14:25). Jesus' response to them was immediate. Jesus knew that fear can move at the speed of light. He told them to "Take courage. It is I. Don't be afraid." Did you catch the phrase, "take courage?" Jesus spoke these words to Peter because he lacked the courage needed in that moment. Peter took courage from Jesus' encouragement. The Lord wants to give us courage as well. Will you take it? Peter embraced these words with such tenacity that he got down out of the boat and walked on water. What an incredible breakthrough! That night, Peter achieved something no man had ever done before. Peter chose to have faith over fear, a decision he would repeat many times as a disciple. As disciples of Jesus today, we can make the same decision. When Peter saw the wind and the waves, he was afraid and began to sink, but the wind was howling and stirring up waves the whole time. Peter lost his focus on Jesus and began to focus on the things that made him afraid. When we focus on Jesus, we can take courage and do amazing things, just as Peter demonstrated. When we focus on our fear, we sink. Courage is something we constantly need to seek and embrace. Like faith, courage can grow. Fear only has the power you give it. Facing your fears is the way to overcome them.

After completing airborne school, I served in the 82nd Airborne Division. In my three years there, I went on to execute many more "good jumps." I was afraid to make every single one of them but pushed through the fear based on the training I received. I trusted the Black Hats who provided the training and followed their instructions *exactly*. I am not sure that I will ever stop being afraid at certain times as a Christian. I am sure, however, that I can always choose hope over fear. I make that choice by deciding to follow Jesus' instructions *exactly* and not my fear. Whatever we follow is our lord. When fear becomes my lord, I sink. I must keep Jesus as Lord, even over my emotions. I can decide to not let Satan rob me of hope by giving in to fear. What decisions are you afraid to make right now? What situation in your life is gripping you with fear? What steps will you take to face your ultimate fear? Overcoming fear is crucial to building hope and ultimately overflowing with it. Allow Jesus to instruct you how to overcome your fears. Follow His orders *exactly*, and He will encourage you.

## Chapter 22

# Discouragement

*Have I not commanded you? Be strong and courageous. Do not be terrified; do not be discouraged, for the LORD your God will be with you wherever you go.*
Joshua 1:9

You may be surprised that God told Joshua not to be discouraged. Fear, as we have already discussed, is a major hope buster and can cause immediate spiritual paralysis. Discouragement also destroys hope but is much more subtle. It can become a spreading cancer that eventually reaches throughout the whole body. If you ask someone what they are afraid of, they can usually tell you. But if you ask what discourages them, they are often not sure. Discouragement is dangerous because it is the precursor for much more damaging and debilitating emotions like depression and hopelessness. I will address several situations that can lead to discouragement.

At this point in Joshua's life, he had many good reasons to be filled with both fear and discouragement. The man he looked to for guidance and support was dead. The Israelites were difficult to lead, and they had wandered in the desert for the past 40 years. The land they were to inhabit was occupied by nations that did not want to leave. Joshua's list for reasons to be both afraid and discouraged was long. Perhaps your list of reasons to be afraid and discouraged is long, too. Regardless of the length of the list or the size of the problems, God tells us to be strong and courageous.

## Disappointment

God's people must learn to face disappointment in a spiritual manner. On our journey of transformation, many disappointing things can happen. Over time, the accumulation of blunders, bitter pills, obstacles and failures can make us want to quit pursuing our goals. Disappointment is especially difficult after hopes have been lifted. Here is one such example from the Old Testament. After Moses encounters the burning bush in the desert, he returns to Egypt and reconnects with his brother Aaron. These two assemble the elders of the Israelites and share God's plan to rescue His people from Egyptian bondage. The elders believe Moses and Aaron and worshipped God. Can you imagine how their hopes are lifted? After 400 years, God is finally answering their prayers! Moses and Aaron then meet with Pharaoh who unfortunately does not believe God's message. As a result of Moses' efforts, the Hebrew slaves receive even more work. When the slaves fail to meet the new demands, they are beaten. Pharaoh's negative response and increased workload are very disappointing setbacks. So God sends Moses back to His people to reassure them that He is with them and will still deliver them. Yet here is the response of the people:

*Moses reported this to the Israelites, but they did not listen to him because of their discouragement and cruel bondage.*
Exodus 6:9

This is clearly not the response Moses was seeking. Learning how to deal with discouragement is crucial in making spiritual breakthroughs. Many Christians today are enslaved to all sorts of negative ways of thinking and behaviors, like drinking and doing drugs, which can become enslaving addictions. The believer can feel beaten down and subject to this cruel bondage daily. At some point, you may have gained hope to overcome your addiction. You may have become a Christian and renewed your hope and your efforts to break free of your bondage. However, setbacks may have disheartened you along the way. Relapse can happen and be very discouraging. Or perhaps you are more enslaved now to your addiction than you have ever been. If this describes your situation, you need hope for change. In the book of Exodus, God performs amazing miracles in order to deliver these slaves. Look how their discouragement turned to hope that resulted in deliverance:

*In your unfailing love you will lead*
*the people you have redeemed.*
*In your strength you will guide them*
*to your holy dwelling.*
Exodus 15:13

These are words of a song written after God delivered His chosen people from the Egyptian army after the parting of the Red Sea. God rescued them, and He can do the same for you. Their deliverance came through trusting God and putting their hope in Him. Regardless of your situation, there is help and hope to free you. All of your disappointments can be overcome with God's help. Decide now to allow Him to lead you to the victories you seek.

## Defeat

Earlier, I discussed the importance of not allowing failure to be fatal. We must also not allow defeat to be so dismaying that we stop trying. Discouragement can stop any army in its tracks. Discouragement will bring our process of transformation to a grinding halt as well. In the past, I took credit for my victories but blamed losses on God. This approach is founded in a deep and insidious pride, an attitude unwittingly portrayed by the Israelites on their journey to the Promised Land. They saw amazing miracles while in Egypt and throughout their exodus but were blindsided by a terrible defeat. They celebrated an incredible victory at Jericho and witnessed the walls of the city crumble by the power of God. Triumphant in this huge battle with not a man lost, the Israelites dallied in self-confidence and self-reliance. Their following defeat at the tiny town of Ai was an upset of epic proportions and extremely discouraging. They were still in the early stages of their conquest and suffered a major loss in their second battle to little Ai. Notice God's words to Joshua after the defeat:

*Then the LORD said to Joshua, "Do not be afraid; do not be discouraged. Take the whole army with you, and go up and attack Ai. For I have delivered into your hands the king of Ai, his people, his city and his land."*
Joshua 8:1

God's people did not rely upon Him to fight this "small" battle. They did not take the whole army with them as they did at Jericho. On your conquest to a better life, you must be aware of over-confidence and self-reliance. It is easy for God-dependence to decrease as our self-confidence increases. Victory should lead us to more humility, not pride, but success can be the breeding ground for pride.

I struggle with this situation all the time. I have found that success can be intoxicating, and my first inclination is often to take credit for God's victory. I have learned that victory is sure, regardless of the task, if I keep relying upon God. If you evaluate your defeats, I think you will also find that you were too self-reliant. God wants us to be victorious, but even the smallest triumphs will not come if we do not rely upon Him. The Israelites learned a valuable lesson that day. If you are discouraged by defeats, evaluate how you relied upon yourself rather than God. Work through your dismay by getting humble again, and get back in the battle. Get back to the plan you had with the bigger victories in your life. God will sometimes allow us to lose a battle in order to teach us a valuable lesson, like the importance of relying upon Him. Joshua and his army obeyed God's command not to be discouraged. They developed a new and better plan to take the city of Ai with the whole army. Did you notice that God spoke to Joshua in the verse above about the future victory in the past tense? For God, the battle is already won if we fight it His way. Your past conquests may have led to over-confidence. This self-confidence, as opposed to God-reliance, dashes hope. Get back to relying upon God, and you will be victorious again.

**Difficult Battles**

The Israelites dealt with their discouragement after Ai and continued their conquest of the Promised Land. As they progressed, they learned many other lessons about how God works, including one such lesson soon after Ai. The Israelites learned that not all of God's victories are swift, and we all need to learn this lesson. With trust in God, ultimately victory is sure. My problem is that I want the victory to be quick and painless; God often has other plans. Not every battle is like Jericho, where the walls fall down if you simply march around the city. One such exhausting battle is recorded in Joshua 10, and its difficulty led the Israelites to be discouraged. God allows some battles to be more difficult than others, so we can become more dependent upon Him and ultimately more hopeful. In Joshua 10, the Israelites want to surprise the enemy, so they march all night to meet them early the next morning. The battle is intense and progresses slowly. Eager to win the battle before dark, Joshua prays for the sun to stand still. God answers his prayer, and the sun does not set for a day. The enemy scatters and goes on the run, but the victory is not complete. The Israelites are close to winning the battle, but the kings of these opposing armies escape. For Joshua, the victory is not complete until the opposing leaders die. The Israelites marched all night and fought the battle for another 24 hours. The army was exhausted and went back to camp in order to rest. Joshua then receives word that the kings are hiding in a cave. Imagine how exhausted these men were after a long march and many hours of battle. It would have been easy for Joshua to succumb to fatigue and pursue the kings the next day. Instead, Joshua told his army: "Open the mouth of the cave and bring those five kings out to me" (Joshua 10:22). The last thing the army probably wanted to hear was the order to "move out." Exhaustion from fighting our battles can lead to discouragement, but Joshua knew that if these kings survived, they could raise up another army to attack him

In the past, I have given in to fatigue and settled for "almost" winning. I grew tired of fighting those daily battles. Victories over character sins and personality traits can be exhausting and take years. God wants our victory to be complete, but sometimes we can stop too soon. Many Christians take this same approach to difficult battles. Right on the verge of a massive spiritual breakthrough, they give in to fatigue and settle for a "semi-victory." In your spiritual battles, do not quit too soon. Do not let up or give in to discouragement. One reason many Christians do not make or sustain spiritual breakthroughs is that they stop fighting when they are tired. Do not settle for making a small amount of progress or making your situation incrementally better. Go for the jugular. Whatever sin you leave behind can come back with a vengeance. Although the battle is difficult and you are exhausted, put your hope in God, so He can strengthen you. Being more God-reliant will lead you to be more than a conqueror.

Some battles we face are discouraging because they take a seemingly long time to win. Other battles are discouraging because the struggle is enormous. We know that we are out-manned and out gunned; the enemy is bigger and stronger than we are. When we analyze the situation, it can be very discouraging. A total transformation into the likeness of Christ can be viewed in such a manner. Victories in ubiquitous and intangible sins, like selfishness and pride, can seem impossible. Whatever battle we face today, someone in the Bible has already faced it and won. Miracles can only occur when we put ourselves in battles that only God can win. One such miraculous victory is recorded in 2 Chronicles 20. We can learn how to face and win overwhelming and impossible battles from King Jehoshaphat. The king got word that a "vast army" was coming to meet him. However, he did not panic. Notice his response: "Jehoshaphat resolved to inquire of the LORD" (2 Chronicles 20:3). Actually, the whole nation came together to seek God through prayer and fasting. During the king's prayer, he said, "For we have no power to face this vast army that is attacking us. We do not know what to do, but our eyes are upon you" (2 Chronicles 20:12b). God's response to this prayer was, "Do not be afraid or discouraged because of this vast army. For the battle is not yours, but God's" (2 Chronicles 20:15b). God later told the king, "Do not be afraid; do not be discouraged. Go out to face them tomorrow, and the LORD will be with you" (2 Chronicles 20:17b).

Our victories over whatever personal battles we face can be accomplished by imitating Jehoshaphat's approach. The king realized that his nation was powerless, and he did not know what to do. He did, however, know how to pray. He put his hope in God, and God led him to victory. The victory came because the king decided to trust that the battle was God's to win. I have often tried to win God's battles my way. As you probably know by now, this approach does not work. God wants to fight your battles, too. Will you let Him? God's victories come through prayer, fasting, and trusting in Him. God will come through for you if you put your hope in Him.

Do not let the size of the army you are facing discourage you from engaging in the battle. Spiritual battles are won with a spiritual approach. What is your approach? Who do you have praying for you to be successful? Are you praying to win the battle or just to be delivered from the difficulty? The people did not give in to discouragement, and they won. You may feel that the army you face is too big for you, and you are right. Regardless of the size of the army facing you, it is not too big for God. He will be with you as you face your foes. Allow Him to lead you to victory His way.

Your transformation into the likeness of Christ may seem to be an overwhelming task. You may be stuck spiritually because you feel powerless, and you do not know what to do. Start with prayer and also consider fasting. Both of these activities will humble you before Him and help you keep your eyes upon God. As you look to God, you will see Him more vividly. As you get closer to God, you will hear Him with more clarity. What is God telling you now? If you are listening, you will hear Him say the same thing He told King Jehoshaphat: "I will be with you." Take confidence that the battle is God's; He is going to win, and you will experience spiritual breakthroughs that you never imagined. Decide now to put your hope in God, regardless of the difficulty of your battle.

## Depression

Depression is a very discouraging emotion and the ultimate hope buster. The sum total of all discouragement from doubts, disappointments, defeats, delayed victories, daunting tasks and difficult battles can be depression. Many Christians experience mild depression at times and function with little impairment to their daily routine. They can ride out an episode of depression and get back to a productive life in a short period of time. Others who experience moderate depression may miss work, school, church and other important functions. These individuals may seek counseling or medication to help them through their depressed episode and can typically return to life as normal in a short period of time. Severe depression is called clinical or major depression. In these situations, the individual often shuts down completely, isolating themselves from others, and at times may feel little motivation to even bathe or eat. They can often feel worthless, guilty, helpless, and worst of all, hopeless. Clinical depression can lead to spiritual paralysis and even a suicide attempt.

Depression is a very serious disorder that affects approximately 20 million people per year in the United States, including Christians. It is a far-reaching mental health disorder that deserves much more attention within the church community. Sadly, few churches offer support groups for depression, and few leaders have training on how to help believers who suffer from this disorder. Church leaders are generally not aware of the signs and symptoms of depression or other mental health conditions, and few know what to do in a mental health crisis or where to turn for community resources to help in these difficult times. To combat this lack of training, I conduct various workshops designed to teach a church's staff, leadership team, and other members about mental health and substance abuse disorders. These sessions are designed to educate them on various disorders and community programs and offer resources for starting a support group.

Godly people can and do suffer with symptoms of clinical depression. Many believers think that a "depressed Christian" is an oxymoron. However, God's children are not immune to difficult disorders like clinical depression. Many Christians do not seek help with this condition because they think they should be able to work through it on their own. They are often embarrassed to talk about it because they think that having a mental illness is unspiritual. Experiencing feelings of depression is not sinful; it is how an individual handles those troublesome feelings that can cause problems. Many Christians are in denial of their depression, reasoning that they have nothing to be depressed about. They see their own very blessed, good life but still feel depressed. This situation can be very discouraging because their depression does not make sense. Depression is referred to in clinical terms as a mood disorder. Moods are caused by chemicals in the brain called neurotransmitters. If someone is depressed for no apparent reason, they are likely experiencing a chemical imbalance. Antidepressant medications can rectify this imbalance. Some Christians feel embarrassed or ashamed for taking depression medications due to the stigma of this disorder. Others may be afraid of being labeled "crazy" for taking mental health medications. There is much the church can do to dissuade any unnecessary prejudice and help these brothers and sisters in Christ to overcome the stigma of mental health conditions. I want to take some time to destigmatize this disorder. I counsel and talk with many Christians who suffer from depression. This depression can lead them to a very dark and unspiritual place. In this dark pit of despair, the volume of Satan's accusations is on full blast. This pit is so deep and dark; it is pitch black. Satan is so close that you can smell the stench of his breath. These experiences are frightening times for the depressed Christian and their family. Look at Job's words as he visited this place of deepest gloom:

*Why then did you bring me out of the womb?*
*I wish I had died before any eye saw me.*
*If only I had never come into being,*
*or had been carried straight from the womb to the grave!*
*Are not my few days almost over?*
*Turn away from me so I can have a moment's joy*
*before I go to the place of no return,*
*to the land of gloom and deep shadow,*
*to the land of deepest night,*
*of deep shadow and disorder,*
*where even the light is like darkness.*
Job 10:18-22

In this pit of despair, the believer will, like Job, question God, asking why they were born and even why they should stay alive. Thoughts of self-harm will be frequent, and this spiritual battle can rage for days. What makes things worse is that the believer in this condition is often isolated and will not allow others to intervene. Those who want to assist often feel helpless because they do not know what to do. Many believers find relief and comfort knowing that some of the spiritual giants of the Bible also struggled with symptoms of depression. We can gain hope from these situations and follow their example to better mental health. King David is referred to as "a man after God's own heart" (Acts 13:22), yet he apparently struggled with depression.

His writings record intense feelings of depression, stating in one example, "I am worn out from groaning, all night long I flood my bed with weeping and drench my couch with tears" (Psalm 6:6). Job is an example of a righteous man who was depressed and sought help from friends. His "miserable comforters" did not understand his plight and accused him of wrongdoing. Christians today can also receive the same response. When believers seek help from the church, they may be told, "it's all in your head" or, "get over it." Even caring Christians can be insensitive at times. These obtuse responses often discourage the already discouraged Christian even more, exacerbating the condition. The Christian can be inclined to think, "no one understands." In these situations, I attempt to normalize their situation by showing the believer that other godly people had feelings of depression. I read these hurting believers the feelings of David, Job and others that God recorded in the Scriptures.

The prophet Elijah hit some very low emotional points and even prayed to die:

*He came to a broom tree, sat down under it and prayed that he might die. "I have had enough, LORD," he said. "Take my life; I am no better than my ancestors."*
I Kings 19:4b

Jonah also prayed the same prayer:

*"Now, O LORD, take away my life, for it is better for me to die than to live." …The next day Jonah prayed again that he wanted to die, and said, "It would be better for me to die than to live."*
Jonah 4:3, 8b

All of these men worked through their depression by gaining hope in the Almighty God. Here is one such example of a psalmist who gained hope from God even in difficult situations:

*Out of the depths I cry to you, O LORD;*
*O Lord, hear my voice.*
*Let your ears be attentive*
*to my cry for mercy.*

*If you, O LORD, kept a record of sins,*
*O Lord, who could stand?*
*But with you there is forgiveness;*
*therefore you are feared.*

*I wait for the LORD, my soul waits,*
*and in his word I put my hope.*
*My soul waits for the Lord*
*more than watchmen wait for the morning,*
*more than watchmen wait for the morning.*

*O Israel, put your hope in the LORD,*
*for with the LORD is unfailing love*
*and with him is full redemption.*
*He himself will redeem Israel*
*from all their sins.*
Psalm 130:1-8

When we put our hope in anything other than God, we will be disappointed. God delivered His people in this psalm from famine and death. He can deliver you from fear, doubt, discouragement, disappointment, depression, or whatever else you are facing. During times of battle, it is easy to put our hope in the size of the army, the strength of the individual, or the horse. These things will not save. God, however, will save us if our hope is in Him. If you struggle with feelings of depression, get some help. Let others know how you are feeling. Many Christians could benefit from professional help through counseling, medications, or both. There is no shame in this approach. Ultimately, God will lead you to victory. In Biblical times, warriors fought with swords and shields. Emotional battles have different weapons, like medication and therapy. Use whatever resources you have, but put your ultimate hope in the Almighty God.

## Chapter 23

# Getting Past Your Past

ᚷ

I love the Bible's psalms because they are full of examples of individuals pouring out deep, intense emotions to God. These inspired writings demonstrate how Christians can work through very difficult emotions in a healthy way. Perhaps David's troubling emotions came from his past: "Remember not the sins of my youth and my rebellious ways" (Psalm 25:7a). Maybe some of the emotional struggles you are dealing with now are a direct result of your past. Horrible things can happen to us when we are young that can affect us for a lifetime. We can also do things to others in our younger years that can cause us a great deal of shame. All of us have "a past" and things in the past we are not proud to admit. Maybe you have many such things. Our past often provides what a therapist would call "unfinished business." This term is used to describe unresolved emotional issues from our past. These issues could stem from something you did or did not do. It can also refer to something done to you. All of the events have emotions connected to them. Addressing this emotional unfinished business can be overwhelming and can have a major impact on our hope for change. The Book of Psalms addresses a plethora of emotions that can destroy hope. I find, at times, that Christians are hopeless about overcoming their past and all of the negative emotions connected to it. Getting past the emotions of the past can be a very difficult task. Look at how psalmists, like the Sons of Korah, express their difficult emotions. These men wrote Psalm 42 and 43, pouring out their hearts to God.

*Why are you downcast, O my soul? Why so disturbed within me?*
Psalm 42:5, 11; 43:5

*My tears have been my food day and night.*
Psalm 42:3

*I say to God my Rock, "Why have you forgotten me? Why must I go about mourning, oppressed by the enemy?" My bones suffer mortal agony as my foes taunt me, saying to me all day long, "Where is your God?"*
Psalm 42:9-10

These psalmists are extremely sad, feeling forgotten as they mourn and suffer mortal agony. They also feel rejected and oppressed. Christians can often feel the same depression or anxiety, but they can become victimized by these emotions. They may deeply desire to change, but if unsuccessful, it is easy for them to become downcast and disturbed just as the psalmists did. When we are held hostage by these emotions, we can also become angry, frustrated, discouraged and eventually helpless and hopeless. Perhaps the psalmists even felt abandoned by God as some Christians do at times. You may be feeling these same emotions now, coupled with fear, in yet another attempt to get past your past. If you choose to focus on your suffering or other negative emotions rather than hope, you will likely fail again. This tragic process of giving in to negative emotions and becoming hopeless needs to stop. You get to make the choice as to when the vicious cycle ends. The psalmists decided to put their hope in God regardless of how they felt.

*Why are you downcast, O my soul? Why so disturbed within me? Put your hope in God, for I will yet praise him, my Savior and my God.*
Psalm 42:11

A downcast and disturbed soul makes getting past the past even more difficult. This condition of the soul can be the direct result of placing hope in something other than God. If you seriously want to change the difficult areas of your life, you must find hope in the Living and Almighty God. These psalmists found hope in God to be their solution. David expresses several intense emotions throughout his writings in the Psalms and particularly in Psalm 25:

*Turn to me and be gracious to me, for I am lonely and afflicted. The troubles of my heart have multiplied; free me from my anguish. Look upon my affliction and my distress and take away all my sins.*
Psalm 25:16-18

In these verses, David felt loneliness, affliction, anguish and distress. All of these are difficult emotions to manage and can damage hope. Some people of faith feel these emotions every day. They often try various, unhealthy ways to deal with them, like overeating, pornography, excessive gaming, gambling or some other negative activity. These behaviors can be coping mechanisms for intense emotions and often offer unfortunate consequences that can cause the troubles of the heart to multiply. The ultimate result is even more anguish, more affliction, and more distress. The final stop on this runaway train of emotions is ultimately hopelessness. As a result of these intense emotions,

David cried out to be rescued. He ends the psalm with these thoughts:

*May integrity and uprightness protect me, because my hope is in you.*
*Redeem Israel, O God, from all their troubles!*
Psalm 25:21-22

David and the Sons of Korah took their negative emotions about the past to God and put their hope in Him. The same process will work for us, too. Difficult changes cannot occur without working through the past. Hope in God will lead you to the strength to deal with these intense emotions that may have haunted you for years. Perhaps at this point in your spiritual journey, you have become hopeless about changing aspects of your life stemming from your past. Problems like character, personality issues, or an addiction can be a direct result of our past. Our current negative thinking and behaviors can also be rooted in the past. We may need large doses of hope at times in order to make a breakthrough out of our past. Hopelessness for overcoming the past can lead to even more discouragement, frustration, anger, and a host of other negative, detrimental, and sometimes destructive emotions. Some readers, right now, are in a vicious negative cycle that is spiraling down and have decided to try to stop the tailspin yet again. Thankfully, we serve the God of hope. The psalmists found hope in the Almighty God. There, too, will you find the hope you need to renew your efforts to get past the past.

Past failures can rob us of hope, and getting past the past can be very difficult. Let me provide an illustration about dealing with the past that may be helpful at this point. I have been to several kids' parties where there was an inflatable rubber "bounce house." At one such party, there was a unique, much bigger version that adults could use. This bounce house had a bungee cord attached to the inside wall that was also attached to a Velcro vest. A daring individual would darn the vest, bounce across the rubberized house at a quick clip, and attempt to grab an inflatable Velcro pole on the other side. Just inches before each unwitting participant could reach the pole, the attached bungee cord would contract and fling the individual backwards, head over heels, and nearly back to where they started. It was painful to be yanked backwards but hilarious to watch. Every person who wore the vest, each more determined than the last to outrun the elastic, tried and failed, feeling the emotional and physical pain of failure.

Many Christians try this approach when dealing with the emotions of their past, but these feelings and painful memories are attached like a bungee cord. We can outrun them for a period of time, but at some point, we are held back, or even thrown back, by the past. All of the progress we thought we were making by trying to outrun the past took a lot of energy and got us nowhere. We are now back where we started with little hope and much less strength. The past has shaped our present but does not need to determine our future. In order to get past the past, we must face it. In order to face it, we are going to need to choose hope over fear, discouragement, guilt, shame, and any other negative emotions brooding about the past. Getting past your past is possible with hope.

In many cases of unfinished business, people do not think that dealing with the past is business worth finishing. They are perfectly content to attempt to ignore it, outrun it, or medicate it. These approaches work surprisingly well but only for a while. Since we develop a pattern of dealing with the past through one or more of these unhealthy methods, we get to a point when we accumulate too much to carry around. Eventually, emotional baggage from the past overtakes us and pulls us down like the bungee cord mentioned earlier. Many Christians have learned how to hide events of the past in the far regions of their brain. The memories are stuffed away like oily rags in a garage. All of the emotions connected to these events are also packed away. This approach may work for years, but over time, these dirty rags in the garage can become a fire hazard. One spark can set off a major blaze. A stressful event can ignite all of these stored feelings about the past and cause a blazing emotional fire, resulting in an emotional meltdown. The individual can become emotionally paralyzed and major depression can set in. This scenario is a breeding ground for hopelessness. Ultimately, the hopelessness can lead to hospitalization or a suicide attempt.

People often develop coping skills, like drinking or doing drugs, to deal with the emotions of our unfinished business. Others try detaching from these difficult emotions, experiencing the event without allowing themselves to feel the intense negative emotions connected to the event. These emotions, however, are likely to resurface in a blowup or a meltdown. Intense emotions are not meant to be hidden away. I have seen many "mental breakdowns" occur because the individual did not address intense emotions like guilt, shame, resentment, bitterness, and anger from the past in a healthy manner. These breakdowns caused hospitalization and months of therapy to get through. If you are in this situation, it is best to get some help and start addressing the difficult emotions that you have been avoiding. All of these emotions can ultimately kill your hope.

If you feel emotionally numb, it can be a direct result of detaching yourself from the difficult emotions previously mentioned. This numbness leads to an emotional void that makes life seem meaningless because the person can feel neither pain nor pleasure. These unhealthy people often lose hope that they can "feel" again and may participate in substance abuse, extramarital affairs, illegal activities, or self-mutilation, just to feel alive. In order to continue to feel alive, these individuals can develop a double life and become hopeless for the life that God promises them.

## Hope for the Future

The past and emotions connected to the past can be very difficult to work through. One scripture that can help you gain hope for your future is found in the book of Jeremiah. After years of rebellion, disobedience, and negative consequences, God did not give up on his people. God sent them into Babylonian captivity to be punished for their disobedience. However, He still believed in them and had a vision for them. Towards the beginning of their captivity the prophet Jeremiah writes,

*"For I know the plans I have for you," declares the LORD, "plans to prosper you and not to harm you, plans to give you hope and a future."* Jeremiah 29:11

In spite of their past, God still maintained a vision for their future. The challenges you currently face may be a direct result of your past disobedience. But God's approach to your situation is the same for these disobedient ones. God also has plans for you and wants to give you hope for the present time. He also wants to give you hope for your future. The past may have been horrific, and your present may be challenging. However, you have a future, and God wants you to make the most of it. God is big enough to help you deal with your past. For too many Christians, regret about the past is robbing them of their future. They are more focused on past mistakes than moving forward. These Christians are allowing Satan to rob them of what their lives could be. Finding hope from God and from others who have made it through difficult struggles will help you to discover the plans that God has to prosper you.

# Chapter 24

# Guilt and Shame

Guilt and shame are common emotions that can destroy hope. Often these words are used interchangeably, but there is a difference. Both emotions can lead to feelings of worthlessness, low self-esteem, helplessness, and in severe cases, suicidal thoughts. God allows us to feel these painful emotions in order to bring about change. Satan uses these emotions to keep us stuck and remaining the same. Dealing with these emotions in an unspiritual manner can lead to more guilt and shame. Eventually, even Christians can experience so much guilt and shame they can eventually become hopeless for change. Working through the emotions of guilt and shame God's way will lead us to become more hopeful. We can learn how to work through these difficult emotions in a spiritual manner from David and Paul.

### Guilt

Guilt has a very negative reputation but a very positive, powerful purpose. Experiencing guilt is uncomfortable but is actually a good sign. Feeling guilt demonstrates that you have a conscience because guilt deals with the difference between right and wrong. Guilt is like the warning light on the dashboard of your car. If you heed it and take action, you will prevent something from going wrong. Often we feel guilty when we are tempted. The guilt is there to remind us to take positive actions and get through the temptation God's way. It is the "check your heart" light on the dashboard. One good purpose of guilt is to let us know we are about to do something wrong and guide us to do what is right. The emotion of guilt also teaches us that we did something wrong. Knowing that we will feel guilty after we sin can help us not do something sinful. I have found that the guilt I feel after giving in to temptation is not nearly worth the pleasure of the sin. Sadly, it took me years to come to this conclusion. Guilt can also help us learn from poor choices that will in turn lead to better decisions in the future. Once guilt has served these purposes, it is no longer useful. Many Christians, however, hold on to this emotion and build what I call a "guilt résumé." They are tortured daily by guilt from the past and present, even finding ways to feel guilty about the future. This approach is neither godly nor healthy and results in spiritual, emotional and psychological damage.

Often Christians hold on to guilt after repentance and change have occurred. One of Satan's deceitful schemes is to use guilt against Christians. Far too many Christians are guilt-ridden about the past. They have not let go of the guilt of the past by giving it over to God. Although intellectually they know God forgives them, they may say something like, "I just can't forgive myself." A more accurate assessment is "I *will not* forgive myself." I have seen unreleased guilt keep Christians spiritually stuck for years. They can put forth a lot of energy but go nowhere spiritually. They are like a car stuck in the mud. The engine is running, but the tires are spinning deeper and deeper. God never intended this wheel-spinning approach to guilt. God wants to get us out of the mud and back on the road. Since God gave us the guilt, we must learn from God how to deal with it.

Few Christians are aware that there is actually a "guilt offering" in the Bible. This offering is described in great detail in various places in the book of Leviticus. God knew in advance that His children would have difficulty with guilt. The point of the offering was to remove guilt and to restore the individual's relationship with God and others. Once this offering was made, the person was to let go of the guilt and move forward. God provides a similar approach for Christians to address guilt. This new way is explained in the New Covenant. Examine the passages below and read about how God wants His children to deal with the very difficult emotion of guilt. I understand that the taking away of guilt can be a difficult concept to grasp. I present the Scriptures here, but you may need to seek additional help to further understand this concept. You may need to wrestle with these Scriptures in order to come to a deeper understanding. If you continue to struggle with guilt, I believe you will find these passages helpful for moving forward in your transformation process.

*This is how God showed his love among us: He sent his one and only Son into the world that we might live through him. This is love: not that we loved God, but that he loved us and sent his Son as an atoning sacrifice for our sins.*
I John 4:9-10

Atonement means that our debt is paid in full. God says that Jesus solved our sin problem. He took all of our sin upon himself, allowing us to enjoy a relationship with God. Some Christians have difficulty feeling forgiven for certain sins. They believe that their sin is so unique, frequent, horrible, or special that the sacrifice of Jesus is not enough. These Christians either have an overly inflated view of themselves or a very small view of God. They choose to believe their feelings over the facts. The truth is that God says the sacrifice of Jesus was total and complete. There are no exceptions. Jesus took all of our sins or none of them. Do not allow your emotions to dictate your theology. You must believe God's truth about removing your sin and your guilt.

Read this Scripture from the book of Hebrews:

*The Holy Spirit also testifies to us about this. First he says:*
*"This is the covenant I will make with them*
*after that time, says the Lord.*
*I will put my laws in their hearts,*
*and I will write them on their minds."*

*Then he adds:*
*"Their sins and lawless acts*
*I will remember no more."*

*And where these have been forgiven, there is no longer any sacrifice for sin.*

*Therefore, brothers, since we have confidence to enter the Most Holy Place by the blood of Jesus, by a new and living way opened for us through the curtain, that is, his body, and since we have a great priest over the house of God, let us draw near to God with a sincere heart in full assurance of faith, having our hearts sprinkled to cleanse us from a guilty conscience and having our bodies washed with pure water. Let us hold unswervingly to the hope we profess, for he who promised is faithful.*
Hebrews 10:15-23

This complete cleansing of our sins allows us to have total access to God at any time. We can now go where only the high priests could go before. Since we are now free from sin, the Bible says that God wants you to be free of guilt. Examine how these Scriptures relate to removing sin and guilt and restoring hope. God wants His law in our hearts. The reason His law was not in our hearts before is because sin hardened our hearts. When we are open to God's Word, our hearts will be cut deeply. God said earlier in Hebrews that His Word is sharper than a double-edged sword. His Word will reach to depths in our heart we did not know existed. We will feel an intense pain that maybe we have never felt before. In that moment, we will have a choice. We can either harden our hearts again to stop the pain, or we can change. Both ways will stop the pain. Hardening our hearts, however, eventually leads to more pain. This deep incision that leads to change is what happened to the 3,000 who were "cut to the heart" in Acts 2:37. The deep emotional cut led them to repentance and to a series of radical changes.

When the heart is cut that deep, the guilt will flow like a raging river after a summer storm. In His foreknowledge, God knew this wound would happen and provided a way to deal with the overflowing guilt. These passages in Hebrews state that Jesus is the ultimate sin *and* guilt offering. Our guilt and sin are connected. His sacrifice was designed by God to take away *all* of our guilt associated with *all* of our sin. Jesus wants to take your guilt if you will give it to Him. There is *no* spiritual benefit to holding onto your guilt. There is a serious mental condition called "hoarding." Individuals with this condition clutter their house, garage, attic and every closet with meaningless stuff collected over years that they refuse to throw out. Their dwellings are unsanitary and unsafe. Hoarders have difficulty letting go of things, thinking it will serve some purpose later on. The purpose of guilt is to get us to change. Once change occurs, guilt has served its purpose, and we need to let it go. Some Christians are what I call "guilt hoarders." Their minds and hearts are so cluttered with meaningless guilt that they cannot move spiritually. They have changed, but they have not moved on emotionally or spiritually. God says our guilty conscience can be totally cleansed because our bodies have been cleansed from sin. Our sins are removed, and God's intent is to remove all of the guilt connected to these sins as well. If we claim this faithful promise of God, we can have hope for change and for our future.

Since our sins and our guilt have been covered with the blood of Christ, we can approach God *boldly*. We cannot approach God in this manner with sin and guilt. When we sin and feel guilty, our natural reaction is to flee from God. Adam and Eve took this approach in the Garden of Eden after they ate fruit from the forbidden tree. They attempted to hide from God because they had no confidence to approach Him. Their sin and guilt, however, did not keep God from looking for them. God still pursued a relationship with them in spite of their sin and guilt. God takes this same approach with His children today. God says Christians can have confidence to approach Him. Christ paid the admission for our place at the throne of God by His sacrifice for us. Jesus' death opened up a new way for us to approach God and a new way to live. If you are living the old way and holding on to guilt, you are not experiencing the full life that Christ intended. Jesus did not come to give us a life full of guilt. If you are living a guilt-filled life, you have probably encountered several people who have advised you to "let it go." These concerned people see the damage that hoarding guilt is doing to you. Holding on to guilt after it has performed its purpose is unspiritual and worldly. You cannot perform enough good deeds to earn your way out of your guilt. No amount of guilt will change your past. The blood of Jesus, however, can remove the guilt of the past and give you hope for your future.

## Paul and Guilt

Imagine the immense guilt that Paul must have had to work through for persecuting the church and participating in the stoning of Steven. Imagine how paralyzed by guilt he could have been for damaging so many innocent lives. However, after Paul's conversion, he immediately begins to preach in Damascus. He then returns to Jerusalem to meet with the church there. Paul had to come to an understanding early in his Christian life that, "there is now no condemnation for those in Christ Jesus" (Romans 8:1). Paul believed early on in his new life that the God of all grace could take away his sin and guilt. In the same way, God can help you work through whatever guilt you may have from the past. God allows us to feel this intense emotion to help change us, not to condemn us. It is difficult not to feel condemned when we feel guilt. However, we must believe the truth of God's Word over our feelings. Perhaps Paul's guilt inspired him to write these passages:

*But one thing I do: Forgetting what is behind and straining toward what is ahead, I press on toward the goal to win the prize for which God has called me heavenward in Christ Jesus. All of us who are mature should take such a view of things.*
Philippians 3:13-15a

I do not think Paul ever forgot the past. His conversion was a testimony to the power of God, and he recounts it several times in Scripture. I do believe, however, that he let go of the guilt of his past. Therefore, I also decided to take the Paul approach to dealing with guilt. Paul decided to stop beating himself up about his guilt from the past and move on. I concluded that if Paul was able to work through his guilt, so could I. Paul's radical transformation could not have occurred if he had continued to hold onto guilt. Not addressing guilt in a spiritual manner will damage your hope and prevent your transformation into the likeness of Christ. If this describes your situation, stop allowing Satan to keep you from being all God wants you to be. Satan uses our past to accuse us; even his name means "Accuser." God helps us overcome our past to use us. Each time Satan reminds you of the past, your feelings of guilt can return. When Satan reminds you of your past, remind him of his future. God wants to take your guilt away. Will you give it to Him? He cannot take away what you are not willing to give up. He will not rip it from you; He can only offer to take it away. As Christians, we believe that God came to take away our sins. Do you believe that He also takes away the guilt of those sins? The consequences of sin may not go away when we become a Christian, but the guilt can be removed. Do not allow guilt to destroy your hope any longer. Claim God's promise and let Him take your guilt away just as He did your sin. Once you allow Him to do this, you will feel lighter than you ever have. You will feel a freedom perhaps long forgotten. Give your guilt to God today, so you can learn to overflow with hope.

**Shame**

Shame is another intense emotion connected to our past, our sin, and sometimes even our present. Shame can haunt us for years and seemingly for a lifetime. Understanding the difference between guilt and shame is important. Guilt is individualized. If I sin against God or someone else, I feel guilty. Shame, however, has a more global, rather than an individual, connotation. Shame is what we experience when we realize the impact of our sin upon others. We feel shame when we do things that bring dishonor or disgrace upon others. You may have had people tell you that they are ashamed of you for something you did. In some cultures, shame is a very powerful tool that keeps the family in line. The fact that certain acts will bring shame on the family can prevent an individual from committing sin. Like guilt, God can help us work through any amount of shame that we may feel about our past or sin. As you can see, we can experience guilt and shame simultaneously. These two emotions combined in a soul can combust like fire and gunpowder. Many Christians mix these emotions daily. The resulting explosion causes a great deal of spiritual damage. Shame often leads to feelings of worthlessness and has an incredible negative impact upon self-esteem. We can learn from David how to address shame. One reason I love the Bible so much is that it describes the human condition so clearly. Take David, for example, as he expresses his emotions in the Book of Psalms:

*No one whose hope is in you will ever be put to shame, but they will be put to shame who are treacherous without excuse.*
Psalm 25:3

In some ways, shame is even more destructive than guilt because it deals with how others perceive us as a result of our sin. Both guilt and shame can separate us from God and others. Many Christians are confused about these emotions and believe they are synonymous, but there is a difference. When I attempt to explain the difference between guilt and shame, I take this approach. Guilt says, "I *made* a mistake." Shame says, "I *am* a mistake." Shame robs us of hope because it distorts your view of you. This explanation of the difference between these two emotions may give you insight as to why shame can be more difficult to address. When our sin affects others, shame sets in, and those we love may push us away. Due to our sin and shame, others may view us as a failure and treat us harshly. Often times, the people we hurt will constantly remind us of our failure that reinforces our shame. Due to our sin and all the shame we have, we may eventually begin to view ourselves as a mistake. This view is often reinforced by things that the people we have hurt say to us. Your sins may have affected the whole family or your church family. Like guilt, dealing with shame in an unhealthy manner can lead to more shame. Dealing with shame in a spiritual manner is absolutely necessary in order to make spiritual breakthroughs. Shame is a massive hope buster. Look at how the psalmists cry out to God due to their shame:

*My disgrace is before me all day long,*
*and my face is covered with shame*
Psalm 44:15

*Why do you hide your face*
*and forget our misery and oppression?*
*We are brought down to the dust;*
*our bodies cling to the ground.*
*Rise up and help us;*
*redeem us because of your unfailing love.*
Psalm 44:24-26

Shame can lead us to other intense emotions and even to believe things that are not true. Shame can make us *feel* like God has forsaken us. His Word, however, tells us differently in the truth of this passage:

*For I am convinced that neither death nor life, neither angels nor demons, neither the present nor the future, nor any powers, neither height nor depth, nor anything else in all creation, will be able to separate us from the love of God that is in Christ Jesus our Lord.*
Romans 8:38-39

If you decide to believe this truth over your feelings, you will get through your shame. If you believe this truth over your feelings, you will be led back to hope. As David said, "guide me in your truth and teach me, for you are God my Savior, and my hope is in you all day long" (Psalm 25:5). Working through shame, as you may know, can be a difficult process. The forgiveness of others is helpful to work through shame but not necessary. Believe God at His word; He still loves you. The others you have hurt may have disowned or rejected you, but God has not. Our loved ones may not forgive us, but God will. Allow God's word to penetrate your heart now, and let go of the shame you have harbored for years. Let the God of all comfort and grace remove this difficult emotion from you, so you can move forward towards making spiritual breakthroughs.

## Chapter 25

# Hope Deferred

❧

*Hope deferred makes the heart sick, but a longing fulfilled is a tree of life.*
Proverbs 13:12

By now, I'm sure you are aware that hope is a choice. Hopelessness is also a choice. Too many Christians have sick hearts because they choose to defer hope. Do not be one of them! Many believers are not even aware that by not choosing hope, they are making a choice to delay their dreams. How long have you been putting off the spiritual breakthroughs you want to make? God's solution to healing a sick heart is hope. Without choosing hope, our dreams go unfulfilled. The good news is that there are major doses of hope available through God's word. Hopelessness is one of Satan's most detrimental weapons. Feeling hopeless for change is exactly where Satan wants you to be. Satan does not want you to feel just defeated; he also wants you to feel like a loser. The Accuser wants you to feel like the biggest loser you know. As Christians, we can get very frustrated and hopeless when we have that *one* area we just cannot seem to change. We can be successful in many ways, but in that *one* area, we just cannot seem to make the breakthrough we desire. That *one* area, however, is generally a big part of our life, and our lack of change causes a tremendous impact on others. The inability to make a breakthrough in that *one* area of your life can impair your health, wealth, relationships, occupation, and especially your relationship with God. That *one* area can cause you to be hopeless for change. God says we can make spiritual breakthroughs in *every* area of our life. Do not settle for defeat in *any* area of your life. Decide you will no longer defer hope, and confidently pursue your dreams.

When we feel like a loser, it is hard to pray, read the Bible, or go to church. Often those with a negative self-image feel as if they constantly let down God, themselves, and people they love. Self-esteem crashes and burns. If we are immersed in a bad place emotionally, we may fail to see that God can still work. This ongoing cycle of defeat and self-flagellation for trying and failing in that *one* area can lead you to hopelessness. This hopelessness can lead to spiritual decline and eventually spiritual devastation. Many of us are skilled at masking our hopeless feelings. In your efforts to change, perhaps you have looked for the "Easy Button" or the easy way out. That is where most of us, myself included, start in the spiritual breakthrough process. Sadly, many believers start there, fail, and give up. Instead of putting our energy into continuing to learn how to change, we put the energy into learning how to settle for being the same. I have been there and done that, and it is not a happy place. I gave in to hopelessness at times and decided to settle for less than what God promised. Settling for staying the same leads to mediocrity. Spiritual mediocrity suffocates hope.

### Hope Deferred Leads to Mediocrity

Mediocrity is a plague within the church. Too many times in my life I settled for this insidious spiritual condition. Christians who decide to settle for spiritual mediocrity generally want others to accept that they have *tried* to change but cannot. Part of this statement *may* be true. Perhaps you have tried to change. The next logical leap, that you cannot change, is *absolutely* not true. Hopelessness for change can lead us to settle for mediocrity. In my mediocre days, I did not want to leave God; I just lost hope that I could be transformed into the likeness of Christ. *Trying* is often our excuse for not changing. Trying is the back door that leads to failure.

Jesus called Satan "the father of lies" (John 8:44). Satan uses various schemes to convince us that he is right, and we cannot change. The master of deception uses phrases like, "you cannot overcome," "you will only fail again," "the 'full life' is a myth," or other such nonsense. Once a Christian settles for mediocrity, they may become cynical that others can change. Satan's lies are much easier to believe and to live than the promises of God. Satan does not need to convince these souls that there is no God. Satan just convinces God's people that they have a weak and anemic God who cannot offer hope for change. If you are not making breakthroughs, it is not God's fault. God is only as powerful in your life as you allow Him to be. If your hope is not in this all-powerful God, you will constantly struggle to make and sustain the spiritual breakthroughs you desire.

If you are settling for spiritual mediocrity, you must understand this is a choice you have made. You must also understand that there is nothing mediocre about Jesus. He did not settle for defeat. The decision to be mediocre goes against your faith and can ultimately cause psychological damage as you attempt to rationalize your thought process.

"Mediocre Christian" should be an oxymoron. Your savior overcame death and the grave. These facts can give you the hope you need to overcome your situation, too, regardless of how difficult it may be. If you have decided to be mediocre, you can make another choice. Choose hope and get back in the battle again. This battle is for your life, your soul, your self-esteem, and perhaps even your sanity. The best choice you can make right now is to choose hope and restart the change process. Regardless of whether or not you have failed in the past, there is still hope. Do you have a pulse? Then there is hope. The choice to stay the same will lead to more painful consequences, more self-defeating thoughts, lower self-esteem, and so on. The choice to change will also lead to some pain. This positive pain, however, will lead to change. These changes will lead to more hope and ultimately make you more like Christ.

The pain caused by change is probably the pain you are avoiding. If you are in this situation, I encourage you to choose the pain that ultimately leads to breakthroughs. The pain of change will eventually have less painful consequences because you will stop the process that caused the pain in the first place. Avoiding the pain of change will eventually lead to even more pain. Did you catch that? Staying the same ultimately leads to more pain, the very thing that you have been avoiding. If there were an Easy Button for change, you would have found it by now. Some people find it easier to rationalize or justify negative thoughts and behaviors than to change them. I encourage you to put the same energy into change that you put into remaining the same, and see the difference. Making the choice to change and face the pain works because it is God's way. The hope you gain from changing will be infectious, and others will catch it as well. Hope is the foundation for growth, change and purpose. When I settled for mediocrity, I regretted it. Regret was the sickness in my heart that would not go away. If you are making that same decision, you know the feeling. At this point, you may also be regretting your decision to stay stagnant. You also know that your dreams for making changes are unfulfilled. God says that choosing hope is the solution to a sick heart and unfulfilled dreams. Stop deferring hope by making excuses and believing Satan's lies. Decide today to get back into the spiritual battle. Get on about the business of making spiritual breakthroughs, so you can be transformed more into the likeness of Christ.

As I stated earlier, I am still in the process of making breakthroughs. As I write this, my father is terminally ill with cancer and under hospice care. His situation has resurfaced all kinds of hope busters. I have many feelings from the past, some pleasant but others of guilt, shame, disappointment, discouragement, defeat, and regret. It would be easy to dwell only upon the negative emotions, but that would not help my future. The breakthrough I had to make recently was to feel all of the intense negative emotions about the past, yet keep moving forward in a healthy manner. I had to gain hope from God, the Scriptures, my wife, our daughters, my mother, and friends in order to make this breakthrough. Making breakthroughs requires hope. Do not allow the past to rob you of hope for your future. Decide today that you will take the steps necessary to move past the past. In this way, you will be one step closer to grasping hope and the future plans that God has for you. As I close this section on hope, I will return to one of David's psalms. Hope in God was the answer to each of David's difficulties: his past, present, and future, and all of his negative emotions. These are all issues we face as well. Hope in God is the answer to all of our difficulties, too.

*Find rest, O my soul, in God alone;*
*my hope comes from him.*
*He alone is my rock and my salvation;*

*he is my fortress, I will not be shaken.*
Psalm 62:5-6

There are many "hope busters" in our fallen world that must be addressed in order to make the spiritual breakthroughs you desire. When we begin to lose hope, our spiritual foundation is shaken. No matter which emotion you are facing that is hindering your hope, someone in the Bible has successfully addressed it. Discover which emotions may be dashing your hope, and deal with them. The God of hope longs to fill you with hope overflowing. Allow Him this opportunity and see what amazing things can happen in your life. By now, you know that hope is the solution to our spiritual problems. Choosing hope is a decision we can make at any time. If your hope is in God, you can get through any challenge. If your hope is not in God, you will continue to struggle. Take some time and study out the Scriptures presented here and other verses on hope. Allow hope to do the work that God intended in order for you to be transformed more into the likeness of Jesus. Choosing hope is a decision we must make daily in order to be transformed into the likeness of Christ. Deferring hope causes us to lose sight of our dreams. What dreams have you given up on because you have decided to defer hope? Do not allow the fear of the unknown, the fear of suffering, the fear of failure, or the fear of success to hold you back any longer. As the song goes, "there is hope for every man, a solid place where we can stand." We find that hope in God. I pray this section on hope has resurrected the hope that lives in you, and you will now choose hope over all other emotions.

# PART IV

# MOTIVATION FOR CHANGE

# Chapter 26

# Marginal Motivators

*This is love for God: to obey his commands. And his commands are not burdensome,*
I John 5:3

God is very concerned about our obedience and also the reason for our obedience. If you are a parent, you understand the importance of a child's obedience, especially when they are young. When our girls were small, I know they were sometimes motivated to obey out of fear. Our house rule was, "obey right away." When they were young, I was not nearly as concerned about their motivation. I was more concerned about keeping them from running into traffic or wandering away in a crowded store. The commands my wife and I taught them were established to keep them safe and help them mature. They understood that disobedience resulted in "trouble." From their perspective, my commands were burdensome, and occasionally they would express their unhappiness with certain house rules. My goal, however, was to keep them safe. I used the fear of consequences to keep them in line. As our girls grew older, however, I wanted their motivation to change. As they matured, I wanted them to love me more and fear me less. I wanted them to do the right thing even when I was not present. I hoped they would respect me enough to keep the rules even when it was difficult.

God is also looking for His children to do the right thing. Early in my Christian life, I found God's commands to be very burdensome. Sometimes I was only obedient out of fear and therefore was not very joyful. I believed God was keeping me from doing what I really wanted to do. Thankfully, as I matured as a Christian, my motivation for obedience changed. As my motivation changed, the commands became less burdensome. God wants our obedience but does not want it to come at the expense of our joy. When we are properly motivated, we will be obedient to God and experience His joy as well. Obedience and joy are complementary, not exclusive. The joy of obedience stems from love. Many motivations can get us started in the breakthrough process, but love is the one that will keep us going.

**Motivation Defined**

Proper motivation is of utmost importance when it comes to making and sustaining spiritual breakthroughs. Many Christians lack a powerful and lasting motivation. An improper motivation may get us started in the breakthrough process but is not powerful enough to make changes that will endure. Motivation, simply put, is the reason we do what we do. Do not confuse motivation with desire. No one changes with desire alone. Let me explain. Three frogs were on a log, and one desired to jump. How many frogs were left? Sounds too simple, right? The answer is three — because desire and action are different. Many Christians desire to make significant changes but have yet decided to "jump." They have yet to follow through with the desire. Some also confuse action with intention. These two are also very different. My personal belief is that an intention is a lie until it becomes reality. How many times have you "intended" to make a breakthrough but did not? Sadly, we can get the same warm and fuzzy feelings with intentions that we do with actions. When we congratulate ourselves for our good intentions, we can bask in the positive feeling, even though we have yet to take a single action. As the old saying goes, "the road to hell is paved with good intentions." Stop paving the way to hell, and start paving the way to change by taking some action.

When I work with a believer in a counseling session, I start with whatever motivation I can find. A motivation like fear will not last. Love as a motivation, on the other hand, has no bounds. Love for Christ can compel you to make the right choices, even when that right choice is difficult. Love can help you change what you never thought possible. To make and sustain spiritual breakthroughs, you must change who you love the most. You developed unspiritual patterns of thinking, feeling and behaving in certain ways based upon worldly influences, so it makes sense that in order to make and sustain spiritual breakthroughs, you will need a deeper spiritual motivation. In the following chapters, I discuss the principle of motivation in great detail. Ask yourself, what is your present motivation for change? As you read on, you will probably see your need to work on your motivation and make it more spiritual.

## Pleasing Others

The desire to please others can be a compelling motivation to change. I work with many believers who decide to stop a certain behavior, like an addiction, for their spouse or children. This motivation sounds noble but can be deceptive. Often times in these situations, someone is trying to make a big change but can fall short of the family's expectations. The family can become discouraged or angry with the individual for "not trying hard enough" or "not making fast enough progress." The ordeal can make the individual grow resentful of the very people he or she is changing for. The individual can conclude, "No matter how hard I try, they are not happy with me, so why should I keep trying?" Often, the spouse of the recovering person can be the "sheriff." This is the term I use to describe someone who oversees another person's recovery. It is very easy for the recovering person to become resentful of the sheriff. This resentment can then become a major trigger for relapse. When resentment kicks in, motivation is severely affected. At this point, the process of change can come to a grinding halt. This same scenario plays out in attempts to make change other difficult changes like losing weight or getting in shape. Attempts to change for the sake of pleasing others do not work in the long run.

**Fear**

Fear is a powerful motivator for any change, but it does not last and actually diminishes over time. Some Christians are motivated to change by a fear of going to hell if they do not change their ways. These believers work on improving some aspect of their life but are generally miserable. Their failure to achieve lasting changes often affects their faith and discourages them from making future attempts to change. These believers generally think and feel the same way about a sinful behavior; they just do not participate in it for fear of getting caught. Their fear robs them of the joy of the transformation process. These Christians often feel they are "missing out" on something the world has to offer. Often these individuals wish they could continue to participate in a certain behavior but do not. This negative motivation for change often creates resentment toward God and even other Christians. Once again, the spiritual breakthrough is not made or sustained due to a marginal motivation.

## Duty

Some believers' motivation for change is their "Christian duty." Their motto goes something like, "A good Christian is supposed to do the right thing." These souls generally attend church out of duty, serve others out of duty, and feel duty-bound carrying out all of their other Christian duties. These work-oriented believers are often legalistic and rarely joyful. Their days are full of doing things but not enjoying them. They serve without the love of Christ compelling them, and their faces show it. Duty is a difficult motivation to sustain. Generally, these believers stop changing and may even stop trying to please the God they view to be a taskmaster. Duty-driven Christians are much like the older son in the Parable of the Lost Son (Luke 15:11-31), making every effort to avoid willful sin but are very judgmental. Their sins of the heart eventually take over and are exposed by situations involving others close to them. They obey God on the outside but are resentful of others on the inside. All Christians have a "duty" to love God and others, but at some point, our deeds must stem from our love for the Father, not our obligation.

## A Better Life

Some Christians are motivated to change by wishing for a "better life" or the desire "to be happy." These motivations are also fleeting and difficult to sustain. "Better" and "happy" can be difficult to define and easily achieved. This motivation is often feeling-based and, like feelings, can dissipate quickly. Believers motivated by "better" stop way short of "best." God wants to give us the best life possible, but we cannot achieve what's best with minimal motivators. Happiness is also an elusive goal. Once the goal is achieved and the individual "arrives," they stop changing, and the progress is not sustained. These believers often return to behaviors that made them unhappy. As Christians, we must understand that we never "arrive." The race marked out for us does not end this side of heaven. The goal that God has for us is to be transformed more and more into the likeness of His Son. This pursuit of happiness often causes believers to stop way short of the progress they could make if they were motivated by love.

Allow me to better illustrate these improper motivations by providing an example. Millions of believers are on some sort of "diet" to lose weight. The diet industry is a multi-billion dollar business because most people, even God's, lack the proper motivation to stick with a diet. Think about the last diet you were on. What was your motivation to change? Was it to get back to a certain dress or pant size? Did you go on a diet because you were you afraid of developing diabetes or having a heart attack? Were you trying to lose weight to please someone else? These motivations would explain why you may be constantly on a diet and continually discouraged. What did you do when you "arrived" and hit your target weight, if you even got that far? Chances are, you went out and celebrated by splurging on a big, juicy hamburger or slice of chocolate cake you had been craving for weeks or even months. This celebration may have lasted several days, weeks, or months. Now you find yourself back where you started again, if not worse. The change was not sustained due to the lack of the proper motivation. This approach to dieting has a tremendous negative long-term effect upon your body, your emotions, and your self-esteem. It can also cause severe spiritual, physical, and psychological damage. I know people who gain and lose the same weight repeatedly. They can set a goal for how much weight they want to lose, accomplish the goal, but regain the weight. They can make a breakthrough but not sustain one because of an improper motivation.

Believers attempting to make changes without the proper motivation are on a spiritual treadmill. They exert a great deal of energy but ultimately go nowhere spiritually. After a period of time, discouragement and hopelessness take over. Instead of learning a new approach to change, the individual learns to settle for defeat in an area of life. They would never "settle" in other areas, but they become convinced that the changes they desire to make in a certain area are "just too hard." The proper motivation will help you make breakthroughs in the areas of your life that are difficult. The proper motivation will help you sustain these breakthroughs as well. Throughout this book, I use Paul as an example of someone who was radically transformed. How could such an amazing metamorphosis occur? Paul was motivated by hate to persecute Christians but motivated by his love for Christ to become a changed man. Paul understood that God lavished His love on him. That love had a tremendous impact on his motivation. In the next chapter, I will use his amazing story, based on the proper motivation, as a model for us to follow.

## Chapter 27

# Paul's Motivation

*For Christ's love compels us, because we are convinced that one died for all, and therefore all died. And he died for all, that those who live should no longer live for themselves but for him who died for them and was raised again.*
2 Corinthians 5:14-15

We can glean several important aspects of lasting motivation from Paul in this passage. First and foremost, Christ's love compelled Paul to change. A compulsion is an intense driving force that leads to a behavior. Continuing to follow through with compulsive behaviors can create an addiction. Addicts do not perceive using a drug as a *want*. Addicts perceive using a drug as a *need*. Therefore, they do whatever is necessary in order to obtain the drug. Paul made and sustained breakthroughs in his life because he had a spiritual compulsion. Paul did not just *want* to be like Jesus, he *needed* to be like Jesus. Paul did not make and sustain spiritual breakthroughs because he followed Jesus but because he intensely loved Jesus.

Now ask yourself this question. Do I *want* to be like Jesus, or do I *need* to be like Jesus? The answer to that question will determine the outcome of your attempts to change. We can make our love for God a spiritual drug as Paul did. Once we change our drug of choice from self to God, we will be motivated to change beyond our imagination. I know several believers who *want* to be like Jesus but do not feel the *need* to be like Jesus. Many followers of Christ would be more like Him if it were easy; I was one of them. I viewed the process of becoming like Jesus as difficult and scary. Therefore, I gave into fear and failed to succeed in making positive changes. Sadly, this way of thinking led me to settle for a mediocre Christian life and a miserable existence. Knowing the life I could have but deciding not to pursue it was very frustrating. As I stated before, the phrase "mediocre Christian" should be an oxymoron. There was nothing mediocre about Jesus. Why should His disciples be any different? Paul was motivated to change out of a deep and intense love for Christ. Paul gained this intense love by being grateful for all that Jesus did for him. Spiritually healthy Christians are not motivated to be mediocre. They are motivated, like Paul, to be more than conquerors. Now ask yourself, "Is love for Christ my motivation to change?" The answer to that question will greatly influence the outcome of your attempts at making spiritual breakthroughs.

Love, as you know, is a powerful motivator. In the past, I did some amazing and even dangerous things for love; perhaps you have, too. When my wife and I dated, I was in the Army, and we were separated by hundreds of miles. I regularly made long and lonely drives to visit her. At times, I would journey the eight-hour return trip by driving all night and going to work the next day exhausted. In hindsight, this practice was unsafe, but love called me to make the sacrifice. Sacrifices such as this reaped great rewards, and our love grew. The more the love flourished, the more I wanted to sacrifice. This cycle works in our relationship with Christ as well. The benefits of being transformed more into the likeness of Christ are amazing and rewarding beyond our imagination, and the more you are transformed into His likeness, the more you will love Him. The more you love him, the more you will want to be transformed. You get the picture, an upward spiral.

Love is a motivation that will continue to grow. If you are married, hopefully you feel more in love now than you have ever been. If you have children, I hope you love them more than ever. What limits do you put on love? If your child needed one of your kidneys to survive, how long would it take you to decide to give up one of yours? You could make that decision in less time than it takes you to read this sentence. You would be compelled by love to make a huge and radical decision in seconds. That is the power of love. An intense and compelling love for Christ will drive you to make and sustain spiritual breakthroughs. Christ's love for Paul compelled Paul to love Christ in return. And this love for Jesus compelled him to be radically transformed. If you love Jesus more than yourself, your love for Jesus will compel you to be transformed, too. Love will call you to do more than you believe you are capable of doing.

Our love of certain behaviors, people or things drives us to make decisions. We can tell a lot about a person's priorities by the choices they make. How do you determine which choices to make? Are your choices driven by love for self or for Jesus? The choices you make will ultimately determine the direction you will go spiritually. Is your life going in a worldly direction? Prioritizing love for Jesus as your primary motivation for change will help change your direction and ultimately your destination.

# Chapter 28

# Knowing Jesus

∿

You may be discouraged by your current motivation, but do not give in to this hope buster. Thankfully, motivation can change. Mine radically changed. Love for Christ is the ultimate motivator and can continue to grow. Continuing to grow in the proper motivation will enable you to make and sustain the spiritual breakthroughs you desire. Some believers need to learn how to love Jesus in such a way that His love compels them. I will take some time to share some things that have helped me and many others make this breakthrough. As I continue to work on improving my motivation for change, I look to the writings of Paul. Since his motivation changed, ours can, too, if we follow his example. We can imitate Paul's transformation by reading his letters more attentively. Paul's motivation changed as his priorities changed.

*But whatever was to my profit I now consider loss for the sake of Christ. What is more, I consider everything a loss compared to the surpassing greatness of knowing Christ Jesus my Lord, for whose sake I have lost all things. I consider them rubbish, that I may gain Christ and be found in him, not having a righteousness of my own that comes*

*from the law, but that which is through faith in Christ—the righteousness that comes from God and is by faith. I want to know Christ and the power of his resurrection and the fellowship of sharing in his sufferings, becoming like him in his death, and so, somehow, to attain to the resurrection from the dead.*
Philippians 3:7-11

Paul was human, like us, but made radical changes because he put Christ first in his life. Christ became the ultimate object of his affections. Paul reached a point in his life when he considered everything as "rubbish" compared to knowing Christ. The Greek word used here, meaning "to know," is *ginosko,* a word that conveys much more than just cerebral knowledge. The word implies understanding and intimacy. Paul wanted to understand Jesus better and to have a deeper relationship with Him. Love allows us to take relationships to a deeper level. In a healthy relationship, the more you know someone, the more intimate the relationship can become. The more you love them, the more you want to know them better. This cycle can go on indefinitely and ensures that the relationship will last. This was the cycle Paul embraced in his relationship with Jesus.

You cannot love Christ deeply if you do not know Him. You cannot know Him if you do not invest time into the relationship. Sadly, many who claim to be Christians know Christ corporately through church but not personally. This situation occurs because they do not take the time on an individual basis to get to know Christ. Knowing Christ in a deep and intimate way changes your life. Discerning more of His heart, desires and character helps you learn what is important to Him and make it more important to you. As you relate to Jesus and His priorities, you begin to realize that worldly things do not matter. Knowing Jesus intimately, not only as Savior but also as Lord, was Paul's goal in his relationship with Christ. He handed over control of his life to Christ because he knew Jesus so well.

Do you know and trust Him enough to relinquish control of your life and hand it over to Him? Giving up control of my life to Christ was one of the hardest, scariest, yet most necessary things I have ever done. Paul put his trust in Jesus because he intimately knew Jesus. Paul knew that Jesus prayed for him in the Garden of Gethsemane as He sweat drops of blood. Paul also knew that Jesus gave more blood for him on the cross. His personal encounter with Jesus on the road to Damascus was life changing. Each person's unique encounter with Jesus is different but, in some ways, similar. The Savior took a personal interest in us by intervening in our lives. This intervention was often unexpected yet extremely necessary. Jesus loved us enough to rescue us from ourselves. He freed us from an empty life and promised us the opportunity for a full life. This full life can only be obtained if we know Him and fill our lives with His teachings.

Since Paul knew Jesus well, everything else gradually became less important. Paul was totally consumed by his relationship with Jesus. Over time, his thoughts, feelings and behaviors became more and more in line with those of his Lord's. Paul eventually gained the heart and mind of his Lord. This same process can happen to us, but it can only occur if we have an intimate relationship with Christ. The Greek word that Paul uses for "rubbish" in the above passage is *skubalon*. This word describes anything that is worthless, detestable, or no longer useful. A disgusting but more accurate translation of this word is "dung." Have you ever seen a dung collection? Probably not, because dung is useless. However, we can spend a great deal of time chasing after and collecting worldly possessions that will soon be useless. For many Christians, the "American Dream" became a foreclosure nightmare in the financial crisis of

2008. Many need to wake up and break out of the vicious cycle of chasing after possessions that will eventually possess them. Have you ever seen a trailer full of stuff in tow behind a hearse? We come into the world with nothing, and we leave with nothing. Paul grew to the point in his relationship with Jesus that nothing else mattered but knowing Jesus.

Possessions are not the only things that can consume us and leave little room for the spiritual. Paul was previously consumed with self-righteousness and hatred to the point that he persecuted Christians. Jesus taught him to let go of these sins of the heart. Knowing Christ radically changed his heart. Christ's love was Paul's motivation, and this love enabled him to make even the most difficult of changes. With the proper motivation, any Christian can achieve the same results. This heart to change can be obtained by allowing God's love to impact your life. The end result is that we continually get to know Jesus at a deeper level, and our motivation to change continues to grow.

**Fill in the Blank**

*When Christ, who is your life, appears, then you also will appear with him in glory.*
Colossians 3:4

Paul's love for Christ eventually led him to say that Christ was his life. Paul knew Jesus so well that He took over Paul's life. How would you or your friends define your life? Here is a small but challenging exercise for you. Fill in this blank honestly:

"Christ, who is my _____."

Who is Jesus to you? How would you fill in the blank? Many believers fill in this blank and tell me that Jesus is their Savior. This answer is nice and very true, but we do not necessarily love saviors with all of our heart, soul, mind and strength as we are commanded to love God. For example, the soldiers who fought for our freedom in the Revolutionary War helped save us from tyranny, but we do not worship them. Perhaps you experienced a medical emergency when a health professional saved your life. You probably don't worship them. I am grateful for the medical professionals who saved my life on a couple of occasions in the past, but I do not worship them. You get my point.

Just because you accept Jesus as your Savior does not mean that you love Him or intimately know Him. Accepting Jesus as your Savior does not inherently mean that He is your motivation or that He is your life. The truth of the matter is that early in my Christian life, I did not know Jesus very well. I wanted to be saved but loved myself, sin, and many other things more than Christ. This fact is sad but true. I had to accept it and take action before I could get to know Him better. When we are compelled by the love of Christ, we can build a deeper and more intimate relationship with Him. As the relationship grows, we will be transformed more into His image.

**Proper Motivation Leads to Transformation**

Some of the believers I work with are more focused on salvation than transformation. What I mean is that the individual is more focused on the fact they are saved rather than their need to be transformed. This mindset severely limits God's power to change lives. Salvation is obviously crucial and provides Christians the power to change. However, the Bible has much more to say about transformation than salvation. We can get that backwards and believe God's work within us is done once we are saved. Salvation opens the door to transformation. God does not want us to stop at the door. Go through this door and see the amazing things God wants to do and can do with your life. I failed to make past breakthroughs partly because I didn't know Christ very well. I loved myself more than anyone or anything, including God. When my wife and I got married, we were Christians. She loved me more than anyone, and sadly, I also loved me more than anyone. As you can imagine, this dynamic made for some difficult times in the marriage. Although noble, my motivation for some of the changes I attempted to make was for my wife. A major reason I did not make spiritual breakthroughs in the past was that my motivation to change was not sufficient. I did not know Jesus well enough to allow Him to change my life. In order to change the difficult things in my life, I had to gain a better understanding of Lordship and the first and greatest commandment:

*Love the Lord your God with all your heart and with all your soul and with all your mind and with all your strength.*
Mark 12:30

For Paul, transformation was about knowing Jesus intimately, understanding Lordship, and having the proper motivation. Christ became Paul's life because Paul knew Him so well. Paul wanted to know Christ and the power of His resurrection. Paul even wanted to know the fellowship of sharing in His sufferings. You know that you love someone when you will suffer for them or with them. Jesus was not an adjunct to Paul's life. Jesus was the center of Paul's life. Jesus was not just Paul's Savior but also his Lord and his model for living. Paul followed Jesus' example no matter what.

Jesus preached the following message from the beginning of his ministry:

*No one can serve two masters. Either he will hate the one and love the other, or he will be devoted to the one and despise the other. You cannot serve both God and Money.*
Matthew 6:24

What prevented me from making spiritual break-throughs in the past was that I attempted to serve two masters: self and Jesus. Many Christians today fail to make and sustain spiritual breakthroughs for the same reason. By now, I hope you realize that you cannot serve both. Loving Jesus more than yourself ultimately comes down to making a decision. More information and insight from God's word can help. We are transformed into what we worship and put first in our life. If you love money most, you will be transformed into a greedy and selfish person. If you love alcohol or drugs more than God, you will be transformed into an alcoholic or an addict. In order to make spiritual breakthroughs that will last, you must put spiritual things first. Transformation into the likeness of Christ is a process that cannot happen without becoming a Christian. Salvation is more of an event. Going from a lost state to a saved state can occur quickly. Going from self-like to Christ-like happens over a lifetime. If you continue to get to know Christ better, He becomes your life. Remember, it is very difficult to change what you do if you do not change who you are. You may change a certain behavior, but if you do not change who you are, you will likely find another nega-tive way to deal with your negative thoughts and emotions. If you are motivated to change by your love for Christ, you will begin to think, feel and behave more like Him as you are transformed more into His image.

I know many believers who compartmentalize their life like the following diagram. Jesus controls a section of their life and may *influence* other parts, but He does not *control* them.

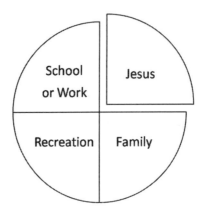

My next question for you is who or what is lord of your life? Lordship simply means putting God first in my life, allowing Him to rule my thoughts, emotions and behaviors. I cannot honestly say that Jesus is Lord of my life if he only has a portion of my life. Conversely, Lordship occurs when our lives revolve around Jesus because He is at the center where every thought, decision and action revolves around Him:

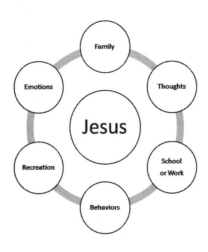

From the beginning of the old covenant, God instructed His people to put Him first: "You shall have no other gods before me" (Exodus 20:3). This command was the first of the Ten Commandments that God wrote on tablets of stone and Moses carried down from Mount Sinai. Later, in Exodus 34, we see how the Israelites, freed from slavery, gave in to fear and turned to idolatry. As long as I had the mindset of a slave, my heart of fear tempted me to put other things before God. When I broke free of this mindset, my life became more about knowing Jesus and pleasing Him and less about myself. I stopped thinking and doing certain things because they were not pleasing to God. Paul changed his lord, and his life changed soon thereafter. Yours can, too.

Paul's motivation for change was to know Christ, please Him, and live his life for Him. This was a choice Paul made every day, perhaps many times a day. This is the same choice you and I need to make on a daily basis. We can make and sustain spiritual breakthroughs when we love God with all of our heart, soul, mind and strength, because these are the components that make up who we are. The more you love God in this way, the easier it is to make and sustain spiritual breakthroughs. As believers, we are much more successful in making and sustaining spiritual breakthroughs when we are on a better spiritual path. Perhaps the breakthrough you need to make is to get back to the basics of loving God first. You will then see that the process of change goes much better once we have the proper priorities. Knowing Jesus in a more intimate way allows us to obey the command to put God first.

The bottom line is that we serve who we love. If you love your unspiritual coping and survival skills more than Christ, you will have a difficult time giving them up. I know believers who were arrested, jailed, fined, put on probation, and endured other legal interventions because they loved a drug more than Jesus. They did not trust Jesus with their difficult emotions or situations and took matters in their own hands. In spite of all the consequences they suffered from making poor choices, they still loved the drug more than Jesus. You also may be currently struggling with a similar scenario involving poor choices and dire consequences. Our choices are based upon who we love the most and who we want to please. It is time to put God first by loving Him more than anyone or anything. In the short book of Philippians, Paul makes over 70 references to Jesus. Paul was consumed with knowing Christ and compelled by His love. The radical metamorphosis from persecutor to preacher occurred because Paul was saved *and* transformed. Your metamorphosis into the likeness of Christ will be no less miraculous. I pray that your heart and your motivation profoundly change, so you can experience this same amazing transformation.

# Chapter 29

# Understanding Reconciliation

At this stage, you may easily see that you have many marginal motivators to change. You may also see that you do not love Jesus the way you would like, and you are not compelled to change by your love for Christ. Many Christians I work with want to change their motivation but do not know how. The following chapters are presented to help you grow into a more compelling love for Christ. Again, I use Paul's writings as a model to follow for developing a more pure and lasting motivation. You may still be struggling with how to wrap your mind around the last chapter and how to love Jesus like Paul did. You may realize that love of self has caused you to do things to compromise your faith, conscience, and convictions. You may be struggling with the concept of God's everlasting love for you, regardless of your past sins and inadequacies. You may be wondering if God hears your prayers, if He cares, and if you can regain the love for Him you once had. These are all reasonable concerns, but consider this concept. At one point, Paul was in a similar situation. How could

God forgive Paul for persecuting God's people? Can you imagine what it was like for Paul to go back to Jerusalem as a Christian after he participated in the stoning of one of the first deacons of the church? Can you picture what it must have been like for Paul to face some of the families he had previously persecuted? The difficulty of facing these situations seems unimaginable but most likely occurred.

So, how did Paul get through all of these intense emotions about his past? I believe Paul deeply understood the concept of reconciliation. A greater understanding of this concept has really helped me and many others gain a more pure motivation to change.

*Since we have now been justified by his blood, how much more shall we be saved from God's wrath through him! For if, when we were God's enemies, we were reconciled to him through the death of his Son, how much more, having been reconciled, shall we be saved through his life! Not only is this so, but we also rejoice in God through our Lord Jesus Christ, through whom we have now received reconciliation.*
Romans 5:9-11

The word "reconciliation" had a very different meaning for Paul than it does in today's culture. Now the term is used mostly in the financial world. It is the process of making the numbers match in accounting. Sometimes it is used in the relational sense, like "reconciling a marriage." In Paul's time, the word had a very significant emotional connotation. The Greek word for reconcile is *katallag*□. This word means to "restore to favor" and was particularly meaningful for Paul because he once viewed himself as an enemy of God. Reconciliation was an important event for Paul. He realized not only was he not right with God prior to becoming a Christian, but he was also God's foe. The cost of this reconciliation was the blood of his enemy's son. According to Paul, we are all in this spiritual condition until reconciled to

God. Our heavenly Creator puts aside all of His negative feelings about us and restores us to Him. This action, performed on God's behalf, had a tremendous lifelong impact on Paul. Making this act of love personal can do the same for us. Our reconciliation to God came at great cost to Him. Paul decided not to waste it on a selfish life. After traveling on his spiritual journey for several years, Paul wrote these words about reconciliation:

*So from now on we regard no one from a worldly point of view. Though we once regarded Christ in this way, we do so no longer. Therefore, if anyone is in Christ, he is a new creation; the old has gone, the new has come! All this is from God, who reconciled us to himself through Christ and gave us the ministry of reconciliation: that God was reconciling the world to himself in Christ, not counting men's sins against them. And he has committed to us the message of reconciliation. We are therefore Christ's ambassadors, as though God were making his appeal through us. We implore you on Christ's behalf: Be reconciled to God. God made him who had no sin to be sin for us, so that in him we might become the righteousness of God.*
2 Corinthians 5:16-21

In this passage, we can see how much Paul's mind was transformed. Paul no longer saw himself and others from a worldly perspective. In Christ, he gained a new spiritual vantage point. Paul realized he was not on the planet to live for himself. This worldly perspective got him into major spiritual trouble and created the need for him to be reconciled to God. Paul learned that he no longer had to be a slave to sin and could have a personal relationship with God. The One Paul once estranged became his Father. The One he once persecuted became his Lord. Think about the negative implications of living for yourself. Living your life this way probably got you to the same place it got me. I was not merely lost emotionally, but I was separated from

God spiritually. A self-absorbed life creates a great deal of psychological problems. For many Christians, living self-absorbed lives is the root of many issues they are facing. As Christians, we enjoy a new life, but we cannot live it the old way. Paul believed that this reconciliation led him to become a new creation and provided new opportunities. This new life gave him a new purpose. Paul became an ambassador for Christ. An ambassador is an authorized messenger or representative. Paul went from a slave of sin to an ambassador of God. Imagine the joy he experienced when his status changed. Imagine the relief Paul felt when he realized that God was no longer counting his sins against him. Due to reconciliation, Paul could have a clear conscience. He was free from the yoke of bondage and empowered to become whatever he wanted to be. This empowerment is not limited to apostles and can occur for anyone who is a new creation. Seize the day, and grasp your opportunity to live this new life as Paul did.

As you read this discussion, you may still feel undeserving of God's love. Our reconciliation to God has nothing to do with our deserving it but everything to do with needing it. You must understand that you will never deserve God's love or reconciliation, nor can you earn it. You must understand that this opportunity for reconciliation is a gift from God that stems from His love. I had to decide to humble out and accept the gift, a decision we all need to make. Gratitude for your opportunity to be reconciled to God and to live an overflowing life can motivate you to make amazing changes. Love and gratitude are amazing motivators that will propel you to a relationship with God and His Son that you may not be able to imagine right now. Out of my gratitude and love for Christ, I embraced the message of reconciliation. Paul implored the Corinthians to be reconciled to God. Implore means to beg or plead; God is begging and pleading with you to be reconciled to Him.

Take to heart this message of reconciliation, and share the message with others. More awareness of your reconciliation can drastically increase your motivation.

# Chapter 30

# The Spiritual Lottery

~

This passage below is a bit long but for a very good reason. Paul wrote this letter to the church in Ephesus about how abundantly blessed we are as Christians. Surprisingly, he wrote this letter about blessings from a very desolate place, a Roman jail. While on a trip to Rome, my wife and I visited a first century jail. The cobblestone floor was hard and uneven. There were no windows to keep out the cold, no toilets or running water, and none of the comforts you would expect in modern-day jails. Yet from these dismal surroundings, Paul wrote about winning what I call the "spiritual lottery." A deeper understanding of the passage below led me to become a much more grateful person. This increased gratitude significantly improved my motivation to make and sustain spiritual breakthroughs.

*Praise be to the God and Father of our Lord Jesus Christ, who has blessed us in the heavenly realms with every spiritual blessing in Christ. For he chose us in him before the creation of the world to be holy and blameless in his sight. In love he predestined us to be adopted as his sons through Jesus Christ, in accordance with his pleasure and will— to the praise of his glorious grace, which he has freely given us*

*in the One he loves. In him we have redemption through his blood, the forgiveness of sins, in accordance with the riches of God's grace that he lavished on us with all wisdom and understanding. And he made known to us the mystery of his will according to his good pleasure, which he purposed in Christ, to be put into effect when the times will have reached their fulfillment—to bring all things in heaven and on earth together under one head, even Christ.*
Ephesians 1:3-10

You may not be feeling very blessed in this moment, but as Christians, we have won the spiritual lottery. Sadly, many Christians are not aware that they are so fortunate. I will take some time to examine this passage at a deeper level to help you gain an understanding of all the spiritual blessings we have in Christ. One thing I realized about myself years ago is that I am a "blessaholic." This term is what I use to describe one who goes through the day looking for the next "spiritual high." This high is achieved through some exciting, external event from the material world. In the past, I have found myself constantly on the prowl for the next good deal or emotional spiritual buzz. The quality of my day was determined by how "high" I got from new blessings. It took me a few years, but I now realize that as believers, we are blessed beyond measure. I now understand that we win the spiritual lottery when we become Christians. The more spiritual we become, the more we can appreciate these lottery winnings.

God says Christians have "every spiritual blessing in Christ." Let's dive deeper to better understand some of these spiritual blessings. My motivation to change my life grew as I gained a greater appreciation for what God already did for me. In turn, this grateful spirit grew into a deeper love for God. I am now motivated by this appreciation and love to be all that I can be for God. Each Christian has these amazing blessings, but too few realize it and give thanks for it. Gaining a better understanding of these blessings can lead to a more spiritual motivation to change our lives. I get the impression that Paul had some sort of epiphany as he wrote this letter. It seems like he was so excited that he tried to share all of his enlightenment at one time. Read what Paul says in verse 18:

*I pray also that the eyes of your heart may be enlightened in order that you may know the hope to which he has called you, the riches of his glorious inheritance in the saints.*
Ephesians 1:18

It seems as if his heart is overflowing with joy at the thought of this inheritance and all that he has in Christ. Keep in mind that Paul is writing this letter while in prison. Sometimes we can get more in tune with spiritual blessings when we are away from physical comforts. One thing I've realized about myself is that the more consumed I am by the physical world, the less aware I am of my spiritual blessings. Perhaps you struggle with this as well. Paul does not make a complete list of our spiritual blessings here but shares enough for us to see how richly blessed we are. My intention, at this point, is to increase your awareness of these blessings with a brief explanation. A greater awareness will lead to an increased motivation for transformation. Each of these blessings is a great topic for your own in-depth personal study. You can use the information here as a starting point for further exploration.

## He Chose Us

This list of spiritual blessings presented by Paul begins with the fact that Christians are chosen by God. Think about this concept for a moment. The creator of the entire big, wide universe chose *you*. A choice implies options, and

God opted to choose you. There is no law in the universe that says that He is required to choose you. God chooses you because He *wants* to, not because He is required to. No one had to talk Him into it or bribe Him. God chose you because of His love for you. In the past, maybe you weren't chosen for a sports team as a kid or for an important promotion at work as an adult. However, God chose you for an incredibly special position, to be His child.

God also chooses us for a specific purpose, to be holy and blameless. That is God's vision for your life. Is that *your* vision for your life? Holy and blameless simply means living a life that is set apart from the world and dedicated to His purposes. God also has a vision for you to make the spiritual breakthroughs you need to make in order to obtain this life. The world may make you feel overcome, over run, overwhelmed, or all of the above. But in spite of your current spiritual condition, God's vision for you does not diminish. God did not lose His vision for Peter, Paul, or John in spite of their many failures, so God will not lose His vision for you in spite of yours. God knows the person you can become and is patiently waiting on you to embrace this vision. God's desire for you is to take the steps necessary to be transformed more into the likeness of His son. Allowing God to love you like He desires is a step towards becoming the Christian you want to be. You are chosen by God to be *transformed* more into the likeness of Christ, not to be *conformed* to the world. Allow being chosen by the Almighty motivate you to do the great things He has in store for you.

**In Love He Predestined Us**

As Christians, we have God's unconditional and inseparable love. Sometimes the best way to explain a Scripture is with another Scripture. A good verse to explain unconditional love comes from another one of Paul's writings in the book of Romans.

*For I am convinced that neither death nor life, neither angels nor demons, neither the present nor the future, nor any powers, neither height nor depth, nor anything else in all creation, will be able to separate us from the love of God that is in Christ Jesus our Lord.*
Romans 8:38-39

The Bible says *nothing* can separate us from His love. God emphatically states there is nothing you can say or do that will take His love away. God's love is here to stay. The question is, are you here to stay with His love?

In the past, I had difficulty grasping this concept of unconditional love and even find it difficult now. Something in my nature wants to earn God's love, but we were chosen before we were born, long before we could earn it. My role is now to accept God's love. My personal and professional experiences demonstrate to me that I am not alone in this struggle to accept that which I did not earn. It is difficult to be intimate with God if I do not allow this love to move my heart. I often find myself taking the Peter approach: "Go away from me, Lord; I am a sinful man!" (Luke 5:8). I can push God away, but His love is not going anywhere. You are not big enough or strong enough to push Him away. I can reject this love now, but it will be there tomorrow, the next day, and the next year. Thankfully, I eventually accepted God's love for me just as I am. My pride, however, wants me to present myself more loveable first and then allow Him to love me. This worldly and works-oriented approach is not spiritual. I resisted the very thing I needed the most. If Peter did not change, he may have been just another nameless brief encounter with Jesus recorded in the Bible. Peter changed his "go away" approach and allowed God's love to impact him. Peter's world changed the day he met Jesus, and he was able to change the world. You can, too, if you allow God's unconditional love to impact your heart.

Many other Christians feel undeserving of this love and also take Peter's approach, pulling back from God, not allowing His love to impact them. We are all undeserving of this love. It is our response to this undeserved love that will determine how much we will change. As a result of feeling undeserving of this love, some Christians feel distant from God. He blesses us in amazing ways with material and spiritual means, but we can still pull back. When we stop and think about this approach, it doesn't make sense, but we can still do it. In order to make spiritual breakthroughs, we need to draw near to God, not pull back. The closer we are to the source of our power and hope for change, the more spiritual breakthroughs we will make. The closer we get to the Light of the world, the more we see the dark places of our heart. The more enlightened we are, the desire to pull back can kick in. Follow the light and let Him illuminate these dark places of your heart. The darkness is where the breakthroughs need to occur. The people with the purest motivation for transformation are the ones most conformed by God's love.

### Adopted as His Sons through Jesus Christ

Another spiritual blessing is that God adopts us as His children. I like the word adopt because it is another way the Bible implies that the Almighty God chose us. Babies can be conceived by accident, but adoption is an intentional act. Your parents may have told you that you were an "accident," but God makes no mistakes. God did not adopt you by accident. My family has attended several adoption ceremonies, and all of them were very powerful, emotional experiences. I know Christians who traveled to the far corners of the earth to adopt a child from a foreign orphanage. For some couples, the adoption process took years and great expense. No couple that I am aware of regretted spending the time or the money to make the adoption happen. The babies at these ceremonies had no clue as to the significance of the event. The parents, friends, and families, however, were all very impacted by this outpouring of love. The Bible describes our adoption like this:

*Long, long ago he decided to adopt us into his family through Jesus Christ. (What pleasure he took in planning this!) He wanted us to enter into the celebration of his lavish gift-giving by the hand of his beloved Son.*
Ephesians 1:5-6, MSG

God takes great pleasure in our adoption. Accept your place in His family. This was no divine mistake; you are His child. Adoption means, "Consequently, you are no longer foreigners and aliens, but fellow citizens with God's people and members of God's household" (Ephesians 2:19). As a Christian, you are now a member of God's family. Allow this adoption to impact your heart and improve your motivation. Within this family of believers, you can also find the help and support you will need to make the spiritual breakthroughs you desire.

### His Glorious Grace

Christians have God's amazing and incredible grace as a spiritual blessing. Grace makes salvation possible. In the context of Ephesians 1, we see that grace is freely given and lavished upon us. I love that word, lavish. It communicates something given in great amounts, yet there is no limit. We have been immersed in the grace that can radically transform our lives. Paul also elaborates more on grace throughout the book of Ephesians. You can easily ascertain Paul's view of grace by the adjectives he uses to describe this blessing. Throughout the book of Ephesians, he uses terms like glorious, riches, incomparable, and gift, to describe God's grace. You can see how enthralled Paul was with grace and why he spoke of it so often. Paul understood that grace opened the door to his salvation. Paul also understood that grace opened the door to his transformation. Paul was grateful for grace, not only because of its saving power, but also for its transforming power. Paul wrote these words to the young evangelist Titus:

*For the grace of God that brings salvation has appeared to all men. It teaches us to say "No" to ungodliness and worldly passions, and to live self-controlled, upright and godly lives in this present age.*
Titus 2:11-12

It took me years to realize that grace also works to help prevent sin. In the past, I understood that grace was the solution to sin. I now understand that grace empowers me to say no to sin. Grace also leads me to be more self-controlled, righteous, and godly. A better understanding of grace led me to more gratitude and an increased motivation to continue on the journey of spiritual breakthroughs. Are you using grace to transform your life? Grace teaches us to say "no" to temptation and "yes" to opportunities to be holy and blameless. There is a reason we sing songs like "Amazing Grace" that seem so timeless and last through the years. Grace was amazing to Paul, and I hope it is amazing to you. Grace can motivate you to make and sustain the spiritual breakthroughs you desire. Grace is a magnificent part of the spiritual lottery.

## Redemption through His Blood

Another part of the spiritual lottery is redemption. Redemption is not a word that is used often in the Bible, but it is an amazing spiritual blessing. The Greek word, *apolutrosis,* translated here as "redemption," means deliverance by payment of a ransom. That ransom was the blood of Christ. Peter also understood redemption and shared these thoughts with his readers:

*For you know that it was not with perishable things such as silver or gold that you were redeemed from the empty way of life handed down to you from your forefathers, but with the precious blood of Christ, a lamb without blemish or defect.*
I Peter 1:18-19

That precious blood was not just a one-time payment. The blood that led to our redemption did not perish at our conversion. The blood of Christ redeems us from our past sins and from everything that holds you captive now. Sadly, many Christians continue to live like they are not redeemed. Daily, they live an empty life enslaved to various negative thoughts, feelings and behaviors. Many believers are still captive to what happened to them in the past. You can also be redeemed from whatever you did in the past that you are ashamed of now. You can be redeemed from all of the anger, resentment, and bitterness that corrodes your soul and erodes your character. You can be redeemed from whatever it is outside of Christ that holds you captive now. Decide today that you will accept the redemption God wants to give you.

## Heaven

Heaven is perhaps our greatest spiritual blessing if you consider that we will enjoy it for all eternity. It is hard for me to imagine what it will be like to go there and be with God and Jesus forever. I read about heaven in the Bible and other books, and I hear about it in sermons and songs. But I still cannot get my mind around it. I am sure, however, that I want to go there. Jesus spoke about heaven from the very beginning of His ministry. He mentions heaven twenty times in the Sermon on the Mount. There are over 270 references to heaven in the New Testament alone. Jesus knew that after His sufferings on earth, He was going back to heaven to sit at the right hand of the Father. The joy set before Him was an eternal place of peace and rest with the Father. Jesus promised that His faithful followers would also join Him there.

*Let us fix our eyes on Jesus, the author and perfecter of our faith, who for the joy set before him endured the cross, scorning its shame, and sat down at the right hand of the throne of God.*
Hebrews 12:2

For Jesus, the road to heaven included the cross and suffering. Going back to heaven to be with His Father again was a powerful motivator for Jesus to persevere through the physical, emotional, and psychological pain He endured. Suffering in any of these areas causes many of Jesus' current day disciples to waiver on decisions to seek spiritual breakthroughs. Setting His sights on going back to heaven to be with God helped Jesus to endure all He suffered during His time on earth. For Paul, getting to heaven also included a great deal of suffering. Since being like Jesus was Paul's goal in life, he imitated Jesus' example in dealing with suffering. I will elaborate briefly on some of the suffering that Jesus went through in His final hours in the next chapter. Paul followed Jesus' example, giving him the ability to deal with suffering. Following Jesus' example allowed Paul to continue to make amazing spiritual breakthroughs. Jesus' modern day disciples can imitate the Lord's example of perseverance in order to make and sustain spiritual breakthroughs as well.

For us, getting to heaven will also entail some suffering. To Jesus and Paul, heaven was a real place. The more real heaven is to you, the more it will motivate you to persevere. When working with believers, I find that heaven is often not very real for them, so it is not a great motivator. One way to increase your motivation to make and sustain spiritual breakthroughs is to somehow make heaven more real for you. We live in such a culture of instant gratification; it's difficult for most of us to think past this life. I do not struggle with the concept of heaven, but I can say that in the past I did not think about it too often. The occasional sermon on the topic or a funeral would take my mind there at times, but I found it difficult to be motivated by such a seemingly abstract and distant place. So I didn't use heaven as a motivator to change my life. Further study on the topic of how heaven motivated Jesus to endure His trials helped me to improve my motivation. Studying Scriptures about how heaven helped Paul change encouraged me to be motivated more by heaven. For Jesus and Paul, heaven was not just a destination, it was a tremendous motivation.

**Count Your Blessings**

It took me years after becoming a Christian to realize how blessed we really are, spiritually speaking. I fantasize, at times, about winning an earthly lottery. I have often wondered what it would be like to win millions of dollars. The things I would do for God with all of that money! (This line of reasoning has yet to convince God that I should win the lottery.) However, God led me to a better understanding of the spiritual lottery that pays far more dividends than any earthly jackpot we may win. I realize now that Christians are blessed beyond measure. I have all the grace and love I need and more. I can share these qualities with anyone I choose. A greater understanding of all that I already have motivates me not just to change my life but to transform it. Jesus once said, "From everyone who has been given much, much will be demanded; and from the one who has been entrusted with much, much more will be asked" (Luke 12:48). As Christians, we do not have much; we have very much. Jesus wants us to use our spiritual lottery winnings to motivate ourselves to be transformed more into His likeness. He also wants us to impact the lives of others by making and sustaining spiritual breakthroughs. Decide today that you will let your spiritual lottery winnings motivate you to become the Christian God wants you to be.

# Chapter 31

# The Cross

*But God demonstrates his own love for us in this: While we were still sinners, Christ died for us.*
Romans 5:8

This very short verse says so much about the heart of God and His love for us. Grasping the significance of this verse also radically changed my motivation. A very important event that eventually softened my heart and led me to transform my life occurred two thousand years ago. Sadly, I was clueless about the cross prior to becoming a Christian. I had an occasional thought about this tragic event around Easter time, but that was about the extent of my connection to the cross. Getting connected to the emotional, psychological, and physical pain of Jesus motivated me to want to live my life for Him. Not out of guilt, but out of an intense desire to love Him back. I wish I could say that my ignorance of the cross ended at my conversion. Even after becoming a Christian, I needed a deeper understanding of what happened at the cross. This also led me to become more grateful for the love Jesus demonstrated on the cross. Jesus did not just tell us that He loved us;

He proved it. My motivation radically changed once I felt a better appreciation for all that Jesus went through in the last few hours of His life. He went to the cross not just for "the world" but also for *me,* personally. I had to make the cross more personal in order for it to motivate me to make spiritual breakthroughs. I find this lack of connection to the cross to be commonplace among many believers.

Although the motivations discussed earlier inspired me to change, the cross convicted me to change. I want to warn you, as we delve into Jesus' death on the cross, that this section can be emotionally disturbing. I do not apologize for this potentially difficult emotional response that some readers may experience. In fact, I am intentionally writing this section to invoke a different emotional response to the cross than you may have experienced in the past. It is a bad sign of a hardened heart if the cross does not move your heart to change or does not improve your motivation. The details provided here are discussed to provoke godly sorrow, the type of positive pain and repentance that leads to change. Jesus' final hours on earth are recorded in each of the four gospels. Growing up, I misunderstood that the death of Jesus was an intense but short experience. In my limited understanding, I thought the bad guys grabbed Him, nailed Him to the cross, and in a matter of a few minutes, it was all over. I had no idea of what Jesus suffered *prior* to the cross. I previously thought this manner of death to be painful and unfortunate but did not understand what crucifixion really meant. Gaining a deeper understanding of the details and the extent of Jesus' sacrifice radically changed my heart. I will share the insights that I gained from my personal study and from others in an effort to help you, too, become more grateful.

The discussion begins at "The Last Supper." This final meal was a very difficult emotional time for Jesus. At this Passover meal, Jesus had the unenviable task of confronting

His disciples about some very important issues, yet the seemingly unaware disciples prove that they are still quite worldly. They even argue about which of them will be the greatest. Jesus, however, demonstrates true humility and greatness by washing their feet. Jesus also confronts their commitment to Him. When Jesus tells them that they will desert Him, they all deny it. Peter was vehement in his protest, vowing that he will never deny Him and will even die for Him, yet we go on to read quite the contrary in Peter's legendary denial of Jesus, also found in all four gospels (Matthew 26, Mark 14, Luke 22 and John 18). Can you imagine Jesus' emotional conflict at this point? The disciples are still struggling with pride and position. Their dedication to Him is questionable. They lack understanding of the significance of what He was doing and what was about to happen. At this point, Jesus could have been extremely discouraged. Was the last three years of His life wasted on overly ambitious and clueless knuckleheads? Jesus does not give in to discouragement but instead takes them to a favorite place of prayer on the Mount of Olives.

After supper, Jesus and the remaining disciples, all but Judas, go to the Garden of Gethsemane. Jesus takes Peter, James, and John to pray with Him and tells them, "My soul is overwhelmed with sorrow to the point of death. Stay here and keep watch with me" (Matthew 26:38). Jesus then goes off alone a short distance to pray.

Luke 22 reports that Jesus prays so intensely He sweats drops of blood. Hematidrosis is a documented but rare medical condition which occurs under severe stress, when blood vessels around the sweat glands rupture, mixing blood and sweat together. Dr. Frederick T. Zugibe, retired Chief Medical Examiner of Rockland County, New York, has researched known cases of this condition and found a link between hematidrosis and the presence of "profound fear," such as the fear of execution. Jesus takes His intense fear and anxiety to the Father in prayer, ultimately deciding to surrender to God's will and sacrifice His own life for you and me. After what is likely the most intense and physically exhausting prayer of his life, Jesus wearily trods back to check on the three "keeping watch," but all these three are watching is the inside of their eyelids. In other words, they were asleep. Jesus wakes them up and confronts them before leaving again to pray. Later that night, Jesus returns to find them asleep for a second and third time. Imagine His disappointment in discovering that these three friends were not there for Him emotionally. Jesus was deeply distressed and troubled about his fate in the coming hours. Jesus tells his disciples that He is crushed with sorrow and filled with grief, but they fall asleep rather than keep vigil with Him. Jesus was always there for them, but in His greatest hour of need, they let Him down and left Him feeling emotionally abandoned. Add that to the swarm of intense emotions He is already battling.

Soon afterwards, a large crowd armed with clubs and swords comes to arrest Jesus. Judas, one of His own apostles who was with Him for the past three years, betrays Him with a kiss and hands Him over to the mob. This moment must have been surreal for Jesus. He may have asked Himself if it was really happening. One of His chosen apostles hands Him over to a mob for a few pieces of silver. After a skirmish, all of the disciples flee. They physically abandon Jesus who is left all alone to face the most difficult hours of His life. The loneliness He felt must have been crushing, yet He continued to move forward and do God's will. In spite of intense feelings of being deserted and abandoned, Jesus keeps going. This mob takes Jesus to an arranged mock trial with the high priest and the Sanhedrin. This group consisted of 70 men who were the supreme judicial authority of the Jews. Here, witnesses falsely accuse Him of lying and blasphemy, and He is sentenced to death. It is very easy to be angered by people who lie about us, but Jesus does not sin in anger.

During this trial, Jesus is also spit on, slapped, and beat by those attending. Physicians who have studied hematidrosis speculate that one of its lingering side effects is an increased skin sensitivity, causing any additional pressure or damage to the skin to be unusually painful; we could relate this condition to how sensitive our skin feels after a bruise, which is also a medical condition consisting of broken blood vessels under the skin. Imagine the additional pain of this physical abuse on such tender and bruised skin. Imagine what Jesus may have looked like at this point; His face may have been swollen, and perhaps His lips were split open. He was most likely bleeding and covered in bruises as a result of the beatings suffered from this group. The emotional pain of abandonment is now coupled with what is only the beginning of Jesus' intense and horrible physical pain.

From here, Jesus is taken to another trial before the Roman Governor Pontius Pilate. The governor briefly interrogates Jesus and places His fate in the hands of an angry mob. This crowd has the choice to crucify Jesus or a "notorious criminal" named Barabbas. The crowd chooses the criminal over Jesus. Imagine what it must have been like for Jesus to see the anger on people's faces as they yelled, "Crucify Him!" What harm did He do, and what crime did He commit? He fed them and healed them, and now they want Him crucified. Can you imagine the emotional anguish in that moment? Can you imagine the anxiety that must have shrouded Him as they screamed for his execution? Pilate had the power to release Him but chose the cowardly way out. It would have been easy for Jesus to feel helpless and hopeless at this point, yet He finds the strength to keep moving.

Before He is crucified, Pilate gives Jesus to some Roman soldiers who flog Him. A flogging during the time of Jesus was so intense that sometimes it caused death itself. This practice is so inhumane, we have nothing in our modern culture to compare it to. During a flogging, the individual was stripped, tied to a pole, and beaten with a leather whip. Sharp objects like pieces of bone were knit into the many cords of this whip. A flogging would leave an individual nearly dead, a bloody mess. Imagine the intense pain of being whipped by leather strips with sharp objects attached. These devices of torture were designed to rip the skin to shreds. As bad as this situation is, it gets worse. After He was flogged, He was also struck with a staff on the head "again and again." These soldiers then put a purple robe on Jesus and mocked Him. They also put a crown of thorns on Him. Brutalizing the Son of God was their duty that day. These men knew they were performing their duty for the governor. I am sure they took no shortcuts as they brutalized Jesus. Their jobs were on the line, and they wanted to make sure that the governor was pleased. In spite of all this pain, Jesus keeps going to the cross. The worst punishment was yet to come. After this intense flogging, Jesus went on to endure *six hours* of excruciating pain on the cross.

With what little energy that remained, Jesus was expected to carry His cross to the top of the hill where He was to die. He could not physically carry it, so a bystander named Simon carried it for Him. Crucifixion is an *extremely* painful way to die. Jesus' hands were nailed to a rough tree through the wrists. Stop and imagine something the size of a railroad tie being driven through your wrists. His feet were then crossed and another railroad tie was driven through both feet. This all likely occurred while Jesus' cross laid flat on the ground. If so, the cross was then hoisted upright in a hole in the ground, allowing gravity to tear into Jesus' flesh at a new angle as He "hung on the cross." Besides all of this pain from the nails through the feet and wrists, Jesus would have had trouble breathing, pushing Himself up on the spike in His feet and pulling up on the spikes in His wrists just to catch a breath. During this time, people tormented Him and mocked Him. He likely became dehydrated and had fluid building up around His heart. Eventually, Jesus died because His physical energy was gone, and He could no longer breathe.

Some physicians who have studied the crucifixion of Jesus speculate that Jesus' official cause of death was "heart failure." I am humbled to reflect on this bitter irony — that the most loving man who ever walked this earth, after sacrificially taking on Himself the punishment for all of my sins, suffered painfully and finally succumbed to heart failure. Even the most loving heart of the Son of God was overcome by the sin of the world. Take some time and try to comprehend the emotional, psychological and physical pain that Jesus endured. His friends deserted Him and left Him to face His most difficult time on earth alone. Jesus endured unimaginable physical suffering from the flogging and the crucifixion. Yet love motivated him to endure all of it. Once I made Jesus' overwhelming love personal, it changed my life. I asked myself, how could I selfishly live my life only for myself when Jesus went through all of that for me? The answer was that I could not. The cross cut me to the heart and compelled me to change.

Jesus' love was Paul's motivation to be transformed, and Paul endured intense physical and psychological suffering as well. If Jesus is our motivation, we can use His example of how to deal with the intense emotional and psychological pain. Making and sustaining spiritual breakthroughs will not occur without suffering. We now have the ultimate example in Jesus of how to endure our suffering. Allow the example of Jesus' intense love for you to motivate you to make and sustain the spiritual breakthroughs you desire. Let God's love for you, demonstrated by Jesus' sacrifice on the cross, motivate you to be the disciple that you long to be.

## Chapter 32

# Attitude of Gratitude

~

Gratitude greases the wheels of our Christian lives. Without gratitude, we will get stuck spiritually, and any progress will come to a grinding halt. Discouragement, disgruntlement, disappointment, and other negative emotions invade when gratitude wanes. Perhaps this describes your current spiritual condition. If these negative emotions were fruits of the Spirit, I would be a spiritual giant. For many years, I lacked gratitude for almost everything. Sadly, this spiritual quality of gratitude is also lacking in many Christians. Ingratitude for spiritual blessings led me to pursue worldly pleasures. I now understand that I have everything I need and more. This new mindset of gratitude allowed me to gain the peace and joy that eluded me in my early years as a Christian. Just as fear and discouragement are breakthrough busters, love and gratitude are breakthrough activators. The Scriptures presented throughout this book continue to convict me to become more grateful. I continue to realize how far I must go to imitate the gratitude of these men and women in the Bible. The attitude of gratitude radically changed their lives and can radically change ours.

One such amazing example of gratitude in the Bible is a little-heralded disciple in much of the Christian community named Mary Magdalene. The Bible records in Luke 8 that this woman had seven demons removed from her. Luke records that she went with Jesus from town to town to help support Him and the disciples from her own means. Her gratitude for Jesus led to an amazing transformation. She was at the cross when Jesus was crucified, yet Peter was not. She was at His burial when the disciples were not. She was also one of the first to know of His resurrection because she went to visit the tomb, but the disciples were absent. She was often present when the men who Jesus handpicked to be with Him in the Garden were not. Why is that, you may ask? I can only believe she was so thankful that Jesus removed the seven demons, she was driven to push through the fear which so often paralyzed the other disciples. Following Jesus took Mary to some scary places. Let your gratitude for Jesus and all that He did for you motivate you to push through your fears.

The Apostle Paul is another amazing example of gratitude. He was extremely grateful for many things in his life, even thorns. His gratitude helped propel him to change his life and persevere through many troubling times. His spiritual breakthroughs only made him more grateful. He was in a very positive cycle that we can aspire to as well. Gratitude leads to growth, and growth, in turn, leads to more gratitude. On the other hand, ingratitude leads to staying the same which leads to more ingratitude. This cycle ultimately leads to unhappiness and frustration. Which cycle are you in? Here is just a sample of some of the things that Paul was grateful for. Imitating Paul's attitude of gratitude helped me to grow spiritually in many other ways as well.

## Spiritual Freedom and Salvation

*But thanks be to God that, though you used to be slaves to sin, you wholeheartedly obeyed the form of teaching to which you were entrusted. You have been set free from sin and have become slaves to righteousness.*
Romans 6:17-18

Paul understood that he was no longer at the beck and call of sin. When temptation reared its ugly head, he no longer had to submit to it. Paul believed he was free to become the righteous man he desired to be in Christ. He was empowered to think and behave like Jesus. Paul was grateful for the ability to break free from slavery to sin. He knew the worldly life he was accustomed to led to slavery. He was extremely grateful for a better way to live. This better way of life stemmed from wholehearted devotion to Christ. This wholehearted devotion will also lead us to freedom from sin. Are you grateful that God has provided you a way out of slavery?

## Spiritual Victories

*But thanks be to God! He gives us the victory through our Lord Jesus Christ. Therefore, my dear brothers, stand firm. Let nothing move you. Always give yourselves fully to the work of the Lord, because you know that your labor in the Lord is not in vain.*
I Corinthians 15:57-58

*But thanks be to God, who always leads us in triumphal procession in Christ and through us spreads everywhere the fragrance of the knowledge of him.*
2 Corinthians 2:14

Paul was grateful for the victories in his life that came from dwelling in Christ. Paul was victorious over incredible sins of the heart like legalism, prejudice, pride, anger, violence, hatred, and more. Due to these victories, Paul gained the confidence to stand firm in his convictions. He was confident in triumph, regardless of the foe. Paul believed that victories were God's to win; he simply had to do the work. What victories are you grateful for? I know that I am not where I want to be spiritually, but I am not where I used to be. I thank God daily for the progress I have made over the years. Do you thank God for your victories? I have learned that it's motivating to rejoice in even the small victories you make along the way. If you set a goal to read your Bible and pray today, and you accomplished these goals; thank God. The encouragement from these seemingly small victories will lead to momentum for larger ones.

### Grace

*And in their prayers for you their hearts will go out to you, because of the surpassing grace God has given you. Thanks be to God for his indescribable gift!*
2 Corinthians 9:14-15

Paul understood the importance of grace in his life. Grace was the gateway to both salvation and transformation. Grace empowered him daily to fight the good fight. It led him to victories and ultimately heaven. He also saw the tremendous impact of grace upon countless others. Grace was one of Paul's favorite topics, and he relished it from moment to moment. My better understanding of grace helped me to grow in incredible ways. Paul eventually overflowed with gratitude:

*All of this is for your benefit, so that the grace that is reaching more and more people may cause thanksgiving to overflow to the glory of God.*
2 Corinthians 4:15

*So then, just as you received Christ Jesus as Lord, continue to live in him, rooted and built up in him, strengthened in the faith as you were taught, and overflowing with thankfulness.*
Colossians 2:6-7

The bottom line is that Paul was grateful for everything:

*Always giving thanks to God the Father for everything, in the name of our Lord Jesus Christ.*
Ephesians 5:20

*Be joyful always; pray continually; give thanks in all circumstances, for this is God's will for you in Christ Jesus.*
I Thessalonians 5:16-18

I addressed motivation from various angles in this discussion in order to help you find a way to love Christ in a deeper way. Once I became more aware of the many blessings we've been given by God, I asked myself, "Can I keep taking from God without giving back?" Let the answer to this question motivate you to serve Him by changing your life. Gratitude for all that God did for him was a powerful motivator for Paul to change his life. Are you stuck spiritually? Check your gratitude level. Are you grateful for all that God has given you and continues to give? Then let gratitude propel you to make spiritual breakthroughs. Are you grateful for your blessings? We have so many more than we can imagine. This may be a good time to count them. Making a gratitude list never fails to make me more thankful. What about your trails, troubles, and weaknesses?

Are you grateful for them? We can be grateful for these things as well because God can help us to grow from them. God can lead us to victory regardless of how big these trials appear to be. We get the benefit of making the changes, and He will get the glory. One great thing about being a Christian is that even our difficulties can work for us. The goal of this discussion is to lead you to more gratitude that will, in turn, increase your motivation for change. A deeper understanding of God's love and grace softened my heart. A greater appreciation for the cross and all that Jesus went through to reconcile me to God moved me to be different. More insight into all of my spiritual blessings gave me more hope and made me much more thankful. The end result was a changed man and a continually changing man. I concluded, like Paul, that I could no longer live for myself but for Him who died for me and was raised again.

# CONCLUSION

Needless to say, I have covered a lot of ground in this discussion about making spiritual breakthroughs and obtaining dramatic spiritual growth. I failed many times earlier in my Christian life to become more mature because, frankly, I was not very spiritual and did not take a spiritual approach to change. I lacked the proper foundation for my life and had to rebuild it on rock and not sand. I conformed to the world's way of thinking rather than developing my core beliefs from God. I was more interested in salvation than transformation into the likeness of Christ. I lacked God's vision for my life and hope that I could obtain that vision. I also lacked the proper motivation to change which also hindered my growth. These reasons also explain why many Christians today do not experience dramatic spiritual growth.

Learning to love Christ to the point that His love compels me helped me to resolve the reasons for my lack of dramatic growth. You will likely need to learn how to love Jesus in a deeper way from others in your support system. I knew that in order to grow spiritually, I needed a heart transplant, figuratively speaking. I needed help from others to transfer their heart for Jesus to me. You cannot transform into the image of Christ on your own. A support system will help you apply this learning to your life, so you can make the changes you desire. You are going to need help with this lifelong task of transformation. Not just *some* help, *lots* of help. If you could make and sustain spiritual breakthroughs on your own, you would have done so already. I tried that approach on many occasions and failed miserably. Perhaps you, too, went down this same road and realized it is a dead end. Trying the same approach that did not work last time and expecting different results this time is foolish. This support system can also help you develop plans to achieve the growth you desire.

By now, I hope you understand that you are not lacking any certain "spiritual gene" to change. Regardless of your current spiritual condition, you can still make spiritual breakthroughs. Change is not a spiritual gift or a talent. It is a conscious choice that we make. God does not need to love you or bless you any more than He already has in order for you to change. Your lack of growth is not His fault. Simply allow His love to impact your heart. The more you feel and internalize His love, the more motivated you will become to make and sustain spiritual breakthroughs. The more grateful you become for all that He has done for you, the more you will be motivated to change.

Now that you have some ideas on how to make spiritual breakthroughs and obtain dramatic spiritual growth, let's explore other assets available to us to be transformed more into the likeness of Christ.

*His divine power has given us everything we need for life and godliness through our knowledge of him who called us by his own glory and goodness. Through these he has given us his very great and precious promises, so that through them you may participate in the divine nature and escape the corruption in the world caused by evil desires.*
2 Peter 1:3-4

I can't think of a better verse to wind down this marathon discussion on making and sustaining spiritual breakthroughs. Through the transformed Apostle Peter, God is assuring His children that we have *everything* we need to be victorious over *anything* in our lives. As a result of this "divine power," His Word provides incredible examples of amazingly changed lives that are still impacting the lives of others centuries later. Early in my Christian life, I was unaware of the magnificence of this divine power and therefore doubted God's promises. I did not make and sustain spiritual breakthroughs because I did not understand this incredible resource or utilize it properly. Once Peter harnessed God's amazing superiority, he overcame his failures and became "strong, firm and steadfast" (I Peter 5:10). Paul understood God's sovereign power and became more than a conqueror (Romans 8:37). Paul prayed for the Ephesians to have a deeper understanding of God's "incomparably great power for us who believe" (Ephesians 1:19). Paul also told the Christians at Ephesus that by God's strength, Christians are able to do "immeasurably more than all we ask or imagine" (Ephesians 3:20). John was well aware of this heavenly resource and became an *Overcomer;* he refers to the power of God 27 times in the book of Revelation. Each of these disciples personalized the divine power, applied it to their life, and experienced a radical transformation. God promises that His modern day disciples can do the same. So the question is; *do you believe that you, too, can be incredibly transformed?*

Before we conclude, I want to give you at least a glimpse of God's "incomparably great power" which is available for Christians in some measurable terms. As you may remember from physics class, light travels at 186,000 miles *per second.* In the time it takes you to read this sentence, light travels from the moon to the Earth. We mortals, on the other hand, travel at what I call the "speed of dark." Comparatively, we travel in ultra-slow motion. The "world's fastest human" can run a little more than 10 meters per second but only for a very brief period of time. God created light to travel at 300,000,000 meters per second *all* the time. I share this small but significant fact about light to help you understand something even more amazing about His power. The universe is so vast that distances are measured by how far light travels in a year, otherwise known as a "light year." It takes *100,000 years at the speed of light* to get through our relatively small Milky Way galaxy. It is estimated that our galaxy alone has about 200,000 to 400,000 stars. God created some galaxies containing over one *trillion* stars. Based on research done by the NASA space crafts, astronomers estimate the existence of more than *125 billion galaxies*. Each of these galaxies contains *millions* of stars, and most of these starts are separated by light years. Astronomers believe that the visible universe extends 93 *billion* light years and continues to expand. This means we must travel 186,000 miles per second continuously for 93 billion years to go from one end of the universe to another. On this journey, we would see billions of galaxies and trillions of stars. I find it very difficult to wrap my mind around these facts, but that's how awesome God is. God's power is truly divine! This is but one example of the difference between human and divine power in measurable terms. You don't need to be a rocket scientist to realize how much more powerful God is than we lowly, weak mortals. As I stated earlier in the book, relying on our own strength is like using AAA batteries when we can use nuclear energy. A power shortage due to a lack of connection to the right power source is one major reason why many Christians do not make or sustain spiritual breakthroughs.

Understanding God's power is also significant because it is the basis for His "very great and precious promises" (2 Peter 1:4). Paul believed God's promises and wrote, "I can do everything through him who gives me strength" (Philippians 4:13). God's Word says you can change *any* unspiritual way of thinking, overcome *any* controlling emotion, and conqueror *any* enslaving behavior. You can triumph over any issue from your past and the emotional hold it may currently have on your life. By God's power, you can be healed of any hurt, resentment, bitterness, and anger that may be choking out your current spiritual growth. You can conqueror any habit and defeat any addiction. You can overcome any dysfunction from your past and face any fear, regardless of how long you have been enslaved to it. You can deal with emotions like guilt and shame in a healthy way, change debilitating personality traits, and supplant negative core beliefs. You can vanquish low self-esteem and all that has mastered you up to this point in your Christian life.

Truthfully, our God is an awesome God, and as our Father, He wants us, His children, to excel spiritually. He is omnipotent and magnificent. He is a God of victory, not defeat, and a God of advancement, not retreat. He is a God of strength, not weakness, and a God of radical change, not the status quo. He is the God of the creation, the exodus, the virgin birth, the resurrection, your salvation, and your transformation. He wants to transform your life by helping you make breakthroughs and achieve dramatic spiritual growth. His power is available to His children at any time for any reason. Ask yourself; *will I believe God's promises and pursue them, or will I believe Satan's premises, my doubts that negate these precious promises?*

The promises of God have no expiration date. They are timeless, waiting on you to claim them, and will be there when you are ready to embrace them. The choices you make from this point forward will determine the outcome of your attempts to make and sustain future spiritual breakthroughs. If you believe the promises of God, you will be successful. If you believe the promises of Satan, you will fail. After years of failure to change and believing Satan's lies, I decided to embrace the promises of God. Since making this decision, I have no regrets and have never looked back. This same choice is now yours. God's power also makes other very valuable assets available to us. We have the body of Christ to support us and God's word to guide us. The Holy Spirit continues to intercede for us in prayer (Romans 8:26), and Jesus, who lives forever and who saves us completely, is also constantly interceding for us (Hebrews 7:25). Angels even serve and minister to us (Hebrews 1:14), alongside a heavenly throng of victors who have gone before us, cheering us on to victory. We have all we need and more to make and sustain the spiritual breakthroughs we desire.

*Therefore, since we are surrounded by such a great cloud of witnesses, let us throw off everything that hinders and the sin that so easily entangles, and let us run with perseverance the race marked out for us. Let us fix our eyes on Jesus, the author and perfecter of our faith, who for the joy set before him endured the cross, scorning its shame, and sat down at the right hand of the throne of God. Consider him who endured such opposition from sinful men, so that you will not grow weary and lose heart.*
Hebrews 12:1-3

Right now, these heroes of faith can be an inspiration for you, just as they continue to inspire me. They did not just finish their race and barely make it to heaven. They finished their course strongly and were radically transformed. These men and women are telling us now that we, too, can get rid of those sins that enslave us and prevent us from living the full life that Jesus promised. They are urging us to understand that failure is not fatal, and we should keep our hearts and minds set on Jesus. If we are weary and have lost heart and hope, they are pleading with us to keep trying because the pain is worth the gain. They are encouraging us to persevere as they did. You now know what you need to be victorious in whatever spiritual battle you choose to wage. You have the information and spiritual resources you need to go after the life that Jesus promised and the one you want to live. *Now is the time to apply these resources and take action.*

One of my favorite stories about one of the members of this great cloud of witnesses mentioned above is from the book of Judges; Gideon's story is recorded in Judges 6-8. God called him a "mighty warrior" while he was hiding in a winepress and attempting to convince an angel how weak and ill-equipped he was to do the work God was calling him to do. In spite of his poor spiritual condition and weaknesses, God had vision for Gideon's amazing victories. God has the same vision for you. God told this future hero of faith to "go," using what little strength he could muster at that time. In spite of Gideon's weaknesses, fear, and doubts, he obeyed God and took steps to see His vision become a reality. As Gideon moved forward, God blessed him with more strength and incredible victories. God will do the same for you. May the Lord be with you, mighty warrior, as He was with Gideon, his fellow heroes of faith, and the apostles, as you move forward to fight your battles, so you can join their ranks and be more than a conqueror through Him who loves us (Romans 8:37).

# Additional Resources

❧

To view the additional resources mentioned throughout this book and more, visit: www.mtccounseling.com.